YORK
MURDER
& CRIME

YORK
MURDER
& CRIME

SUMMER STREVENS

First published 2013

The History Press
The Mill, Brimscombe Port
Stroud, Gloucestershire, GL5 2QG
www.thehistorypress.co.uk

British Library Cataloguing in Publication Data.
A catalogue record for this book is available from the British Library.

ISBN 978 0 7524 7482 3

Typesetting and origination by The History Press
Printed in Great Britain

CONTENTS

INTRODUCTION

Peculiar as it may seem, it is still legal to kill a Scotsman within the city walls of York, so long as your chosen weapon is a longbow and you don't shoot on a Sunday! Just one of the many historic un-repealed laws still remaining on the statute book; though it may seem nonsensical today, at the time this law was passed it was considered expedient legislation in the face of the repeated Scottish raiding parties, terrorising York after the defeat of Edward II's army at the Battle of Bannockburn in 1314.

York's history is long and colourful, reflected in the street pattern of the city that still thrives within the confines of its walls, evolving from the Roman Eboracum to the seventh-century Anglian Eoforwic then the Viking Jorvik, and while the York of the Middle Ages is all but hidden and disguised beneath Georgian and Victorian façades, the fabric of the city is almost entirely medieval underneath it all.

In the 1720s, Daniel Defoe wrote of the city in his *A Tour Thro' The Whole Island Of Great Britain* that, 'Fires, sieges, plunderings and devastations, have often been the fate of York; so that one should wonder there should be any thing of a city left.'

The glorious York Minster was once juxtaposed with streetscapes of noisy and crowded narrow lanes crammed full of dwellings – a far cry from today's York. It was smelly too! Butchers' offal rotted in the street, and where privies didn't empty into the city moat or over the Ouse Bridge, slops were destined for the street; little wonder then that in the fourteenth century, York was ranked amongst the filthiest of cities. In a letter from Edward III to the Mayor and bailiffs of York in 1332, Edward, who knew York well, complained of 'dung and manure wherewith the streets and lanes are filled and obstructed.' In spite of a number of ordinances passed stating that pigs, prostitutes and all manner of excrement were no longer to be tolerated on the street, the lane called Patrick's Pool, a continuation of Swinegate, was described in 1249 as 'so deep in mire that it was impassable'.

The social situation with regard to overcrowding, filth and disease was further exacerbated in the late eighteenth century, when the population swelled from 17,000 inhabitants in the year 1800 to 40,000 by 1850. This increase inevitably spawned dark and overrun tenements in certain districts of the city, which in turn bred crime and disorder. The three Waters lanes of the city (though swept away by a flush of Victorian development in 1881 creating King Street, Cumberland Street and Clifford Street) overlay a former neighbourhood of the poorest classes, known for housing the desperate and the poor, including many of York's population of prostitutes. Large families were forced to live in back-to-back courtyard dwellings sharing a single standpipe and one midden privy – no small wonder, then, that in 1831 the unfortunates from just those three streets alone accounted for 10 per cent of all the cholera deaths suffered in the epidemic of that year. Naturally, theft and violent crime was rife in these areas and dealt with harshly. Writing in 1856, Charles Phillips, Barrister & Commissioner for the Court of Insolvent Debtors, remarked that, 'We hanged for anything – for a shilling – for five pounds – for cattle – for coining – for forgery, even witchcraft – for things that were and things that could not be.'

Of course, York today is a healthy and vibrant city. However, there are reminders everywhere harking back to its more discordant past; if one enters where the road pierces the city walls at Monk Bar, if you look above as you pass beneath the fourteenth-century four-storey gatehouse you will see the crude limestone figures positioned around the top of the crenulated turrets, poised to drop rocks on the heads of any potential miscreants entering the city.

In this book, I have drawn together what I hope will prove an interesting and varied set of accounts of murders and crimes, of punishment, incarceration and executions in York. From treason, insurrection and highway robbery to plain old theft and slander, all were viewed as transgressions in the eyes of the law and treated as such, and invariably with decisive finality.

Rather than scrolling off a litany of criminals and their crimes in a staid chronology of York's darker past, I have tried to give a flavour of the everyday as well as the notorious. While some of the higher profile murders and crimes mentioned herein may not have actually been perpetrated within the city walls, I hope that the reader will forgive me for straying outside of the city boundaries, as every soul included in these pages, regardless of the geographical specifics of their transgression, was either tried, imprisoned, punished or ultimately executed in York itself. Their accounts are too interesting and poignant to exclude on the pretext that they may deviate from strict titular adherence – they do, after all, form part of the fabric of York's judicial history.

I hope you will enjoy this collection of some of the foulest deeds perpetrated and punished in York's past, uncovered from the often overlooked shadier side of this city's character. With stories ranging from child murders to brutal stabbings, the transgressions that are revealed promise to shock and fascinate in equal measure.

I would like to acknowledge and offer my grateful thanks to all those who have assisted with the writing of this book. To Jack Gritton especially for the photography; Michael Woodward of York Museums Trust for his patience in the face of my interminable permission and copyright enquiries, along with the staff of York Castle Museum, and Ian Drake, Keeper of the Evelyn Collection for The Yorkshire Architectural & York Archaeological Society.

Whether your interests lay in true crime or historic York itself, I hope you will enjoy the accounts that follow as much as I have enjoyed researching and writing about them.

Summer Strevens, 2013

CHAPTER ONE

YORK'S GAOLS

In the heart of old York, and probably the oldest candidate as a site of incarceration, stands Clifford's Tower. The tower is almost all that now remains of York Castle, originally built by William the Conqueror in 1068. Sited on the defensible vantage of a tall mound and offering panoramic views out over the historic city, Clifford's Tower is surely one of the most popular and iconic of York's historic attractions today. In 1190 the tower was the scene of a tragedy fuelled by anti-Semitism that is remembered still and commemorated with the memorial stone at the base of the castle mound. In fact, it is said that the ground within the tower is still stained red, even after being dug up and replaced.

Clifford's Tower, York.

Memorial Stone commemorating the deaths of some 150 Jews who were massacred in a pogrom in the castle keep in 1190.

William the Conqueror built two castles in York; the second, known as the Olde Baile, was built in 1069, across from its counterpart on the River Ouse. Both constructed as motte and bailey fortifications, they were sited so that a chain could be slung across the river between the two, in order to prevent a repeat of Norwegian King Harold Hadrada's watery attack some three years previously. Like York Castle, the Old Baile was also used as a gaol, passing into the ownership of the Archbishop of York in 1194 and thereafter known as the Archbishops' Castle, with part of the defences evocatively named Bitch Daughter Tower and used as a royal prison. Though undergoing various changes of use over time, with the upper storeys providing a ready supply of stone when the Ouse Bridge was in need of repair in 1567, Bitch Daughter Tower was also utilised as a guardhouse during the Parliamentary siege of York in 1644. By the nineteenth century however, it had fallen into use as a lowly stable.

Written records attest to York Castle being used as a gaol from the earliest times, and it was certainly employed as such during the troubled reign of King John from 1199 to 1216. While the keep of the castle formed the royal quarters, providing for John's own security, prisoners taken during the King's Irish campaigns were also held there. In the reign of John's successor,

King Henry III, York Castle's role as a gaol was expanded to hold a wide range of prisoners, with over 300 inmates incarcerated at any one time in what were described as 'appalling' conditions, often resulting in death during imprisonment. Responsibility for the gaol during this period fell to the Sheriff, but his deputy usually filled the role of full-time gaoler; though the efficacy of the deputy in charge during 1298 must be open to question, as twenty-eight prisoners successfully broke out in this year. In 1307, York Castle was used to hold many of the arrested Knights Templar on the dissolution of their military order, and in 1322 King Edward II also used the castle as a repository for rebellious barons taken prisoner during his reprisal campaign, many of whom, following his victory at the Battle of Boroughbridge, were executed there.

York Castle continued to be used extensively as a gaol, with prisoners distributed around the various towers surrounding the bailey, although during Cromwell's Commonwealth, efforts were made to separate Clifford's Tower (which Parliament was using as a garrison) from the bailey buildings, which continued to be used as a prison. Political prisoners continued to be

Bitch Daughter Tower.

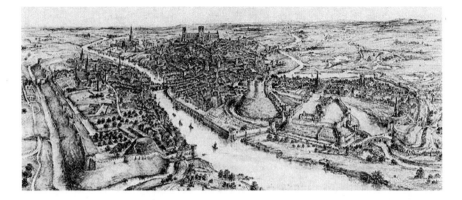

A panorama of fifteenth-century York by E. Ridsdale Tate. York Castle is on the right-hand side of river, opposite the abandoned motte of Baile Hill. (Courtesy of York Museums Trust, York Art Gallery)

held in the castle after the Restoration, most notably George Fox, founder of the Society of Friends.

As one might expect, the York authorities also controlled a number of municipal premises for the purposes of penitentiary, and the first solid reference to a public prison granted by the Crown is in 1278–9, when the Kidcote is mentioned. (The Close Rolls – the Chancery's administrative records of the time – do allude to such a prison earlier on in 1248, however.) The origin of this name is uncertain but it may well have been a facetious nickname, as the literal meaning of kidcote is 'A pen used to confine young goats', and the use of the name seems more prevalent in the north, with Lancaster, Wakefield, Lincoln and Gainsborough all boasting Kidcotes.

Guarded by bailiffs during the day and the city's butchers at night, the Kidcote was used to confine detainees of both sexes before they could be brought before a court. Mere suspicion of being a 'night walker' could prove strong enough grounds for being locked up; in other words, if one was found to be out after dark and deemed to be of dubious appearance, then there was a good chance of spending some time in the Kidcote. It would seem that by 1398 York had a need for increased holding capacity, as there are references to more than one Kidcote. Numbering at least seven, it is known that two of these, the Sheriffs' Prison and the Mayor's Prison, were in operation. These were sited at either end of the medieval Ouse Bridge, and while conditions must have been squalid at the best of times,

A panorama of York Castle (c. 1730). (Courtesy of York Museums Trust, York Art Gallery)

the situation must have been considerably worsened when the river flooded. The Ouse did and still does flood frequently, but the flooding in the winter of 1564–65 caused part of the bridge to be swept away.

In York, certain Kidcotes were used by various authorities, depending on the specific transgression committed. The differentiation in the criminal criteria determining which Kidcote was used to hold which offenders is not entirely clear cut; however, as an example, a man charged with stealing the keys of Bootham Bar in 1489 was held in the Sheriffs' custody, as was a suspected murderer in 1522, while another man accused of posting 'slanderous bills' in 1536 was detained at the other end of the bridge, in the Mayor's Kidcote.

York can also lay claim to being the only city on historical record to have ever had a dedicated 'forest prison'. Located on Davygate in a building called Davy Hall, this lock-up was used exclusively to hold those who had broken Forest Law, a harsh legislation introduced by the first of England's Norman kings, William the Conqueror. Operating outside of Common Law, it was intended to protect and preserve the level of animals in newly designated Royal Forests from lowly poachers, to ensure a plentiful supply could be hunted exclusively for royal pleasure. Appropriately enough, Davy Hall was

Ouse Bridge in 1791, by artist John White Abbott. (Courtesy of York Museums Trust, York Art Gallery)

administered by the king's Larderer, who was responsible for ensuring sufficient fresh meat a-plenty was available for royal consumption whenever the monarch visited York. The first royal records which mention the Larderer, in 1135, show that his name was David; his descendants, usually called David, were to remain in this hereditary role until the fifteenth century.

Surprisingly, even York Minster had its own prison, though this was exclusively for holding clerical lawbreakers. In view of the more relaxed punishments meted out to the clergy in their own church courts, it was commonplace for accused criminals to try to 'plead clergy', claiming to be a churchman and thereby eligible to be tried by the ecclesiastic courts and hopefully receiving more lenient treatment. Known as the Bishop Prison, or latterly the Convict Prison, the Archbishop's gaol was in operation by 1351. Located in the precincts of the Archbishop's Palace, most probably in the crypt of St Sepulchre's Chapel, it has been mooted that a possible alternative site for this prison was within the Old Baile, however, in 1816, during the

Ouse Bridge as it appears today, without the Kidcotes.

rebuilding of The Hole in the Wall pub, the discovery of an underground room measuring 32ft by 9ft was made beneath the building, lending weight to the prior claim that St Sepulchre's had in fact been somewhat irreverently converted into a public house.

The Church's custodial reach also extended to its tenants, over whom it exercised independent jurisdiction. Both St Mary's Abbey and the Minster exercised control over all that went on within their own walled boundaries, the areas inside known as the Liberty of St Mary and the Liberty of St Peter respectively, hence York Minster's very own gaol and gallows are known as 'Peter Prison'. The first mention of 'Seyntepetreprisons', as Peter Prison was sometimes known, is in 1275 and was initially sited where Stonegate enters the Minster Yard (now Minster Gates, Deangate). Later, at some unspecified date, the prison was relocated to a site that lay within the Lop Lane gate of the Minster precincts, and the York Arms public house in High Petergate now lays claim to occupying the former site of Peter Prison.

By 1289, St Mary's Abbey Prison, the sister gaol to Peter Prison, was built. The abbey's right to keep the prison was expressly granted by charter in 1448 and despite the dissolution of King Henry VIII's reign, the Liberty of

St Mary's Abbey was preserved along with its privileges, which included the maintenance of a debtors' prison located beside the abbey's north gate. However, by 1736, records show that the prison and adjacent courtroom were in a 'neglected' state and it can be assumed that use of the premises were curtailed from this time, if not before. Ironically, stone from the ruins of St Mary's Abbey was used in the construction of the new County Prison, completed in 1705.

Davygate, York.

In addition to these church prisons and various Kidcotes, other prisons did exist in the city. One such was located close to the city moat, in the area known as Bean Hills, midway between Fishergate and Walmgate bars ('Bars' being the name given to the imposing gateways punctuating the city's impressive walls, all four are still in existence today). It is likely that the actual guardroom of Fishergate Bar (later known as Bean Hills gate) was used to imprison both sexes who were held as 'recusants' – nonconformist Roman Catholics in the reign of Elizabeth I – and by 1577 the surge in their persecution necessitated the use of the gatehouse of Monk Bar as a prison as well, with the addition of a new prison on the King's Staith, built in 1585.

By 1609, overcrowding in York Castle Gaol had reached such a level that prisoners were being pardoned and released, in order to make room for the new detainees. By 1636, however, the gaol had fallen into such a state of decay that several attempts to escape were successfully made in the following years. Most notably by James Willas who, having been imprisoned in September 1731 for house breaking, escaped from York Castle Gaol twice, and on his second attempt absconded with twenty-one other felons. In the wanted notice that was issued after his first, ultimately unsuccessful escape in November 1731, Willas was described as 'A Felon, late of Doncaster, a broad well-set Man, black down-looking Complexion, middle-siz'd, pock-ared [sic], wears a black Wig'. Of the eighteen felons who were recaptured after the second escape, ten were subsequently hanged, Willas among them.

Another ambitious but failed escape attempt was made by George Harger in September 1761. Committed for murder, Harger sought to dig his way out of the castle with a knife and a shoemaker's hammer – he was discovered several yards underground and afterwards was chained to the wall with his three accomplices, John Wilson, William Andrews and George Cox.

Presumably the long inadequate holding facilities were the catalyst for the decision in 1701 to build a new prison in the bailey area of York Castle. Though the chronology above attests that the castle still functioned as a gaol, the old buildings were swept away (apart from Clifford's Tower) and the new County Gaol was open by 1705. Known as the Debtors' Prison and described by Daniel Defoe as 'The most stately and complete prison of any in the Kingdom, if not in Europe, kept as neat within side as it is noble without', the prison actually became a visitor attraction in its own right; the gentry classes would come to view the prisoners through the railings of the exercise yard. All classes and classification of criminal were visible; murderers and malcontents, bigamists and burglars, poisoners and prostitutes. For example, murderer William Meyer, a native of York, was held here. He had been found guilty of shooting dead Joseph Spink, assistant to the Sheriff's office. Meyer murdered Spink in his own home in Micklegate on 18 October 1780. At his trial held at York Lent Assizes, Meyer's wife Mary was acquitted of involvement with the murder; Meyer was hanged on 6 April 1781.

Being found guilty for burglary also carried the death penalty. In 1579, ringleader Charles de Pascal and four accomplices (Thomas de Warltire, aged twenty-nine; George de Priestly, aged forty; Hannah Fourcroy, aged twenty-five and Charlotte Morrett, aged twenty-seven) were all executed on July 30 for breaking into the warehouse of Mr Robert Kirwan and stealing silks and drapery goods to the value of 100 guineas – in today's money, the value of the stolen goods amounted to just shy of £20,000.

In 1783, John Riley, native of York, under the cover of darkness broke into Peter Pollard's house in St Helen's, Stonegate and made off with

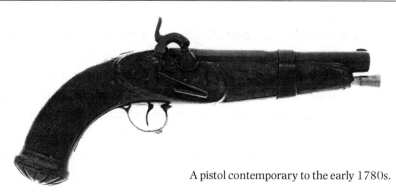

A pistol contemporary to the early 1780s.

380 yards of linen, worth an estimated 17 guineas – Riley was found guilty at Summer Assizes and hanged on Saturday, 23 August 1783.

Although not as well known as Dick Turpin, fellow highwayman William Brown still suffered the ultimate penalty of the law when found guilty of robbery on York's fashionable New Walk. He was charged for the savage and aggravated theft from John Armstrong, who was in fact a neighbour of Brown's. The presiding judge, Mr Raine, passed sentence without 'a shadow of mercy', and the jury took only three minutes to return with a verdict of 'guilty'. Brown was executed at the New Drop on 20 August 1809.

For a while, the new prison served its purpose well. In the early years of the eighteenth century, records indicate that the prison buildings were kept clean and that a chaplain and surgeon were employed there, even before the introduction of compulsory legislation to do so. However, John Howard,

'savage and aggravated theft'

'the Great Prison Reformer of the eighteenth century', visited York Prison in the early 1780s and found it, 'A noisesome place with cells that were little more than unlighted dungeons, and, thanks to those who inhabited them, filth and fever-haunted dens of iniquity in which hundreds of people in festering masses were confined.'

The prisoners were given a 3lb 2oz loaf every Tuesday and Friday, and this was all they would have to eat unless they had friends or relatives who brought them food. The tiny cells were 7ft by 6ft, with only straw on the floor for bedding. There was an open sewer running along the passages, but no water in the cells. Each cell usually held up to three prisoners, but not everyone convicted of a capital offence made it to the gallows. Prisoners were often tightly packed into the cells and on the night of 27 October 1737 nine prisoners confined in the same cell actually suffocated to death. Prisoners were, however, allowed to exercise daily in the prison courtyard and while doing so they were afforded the opportunity of talking to their friends and relations on the outside.

Yet in spite of these conditions, one man actually pleaded for a cell in the prison over being kept at the York Asylum. The sorry case of Frank Parker who had been committed to the asylum in April 1837 highlights the unhappy situation for some of those suffering mental illness in the eighteenth century. In spite of having his hands fastened to his side to prevent him from harming himself, Parker still managed to kick fellow 'lunatic' Thomas Ward to death, who Parker was convinced had been sent to the asylum specifically to kill him, and as he stated at his trial he 'got in first'. He also maintained that he had been unlawfully detained, while stating 'I should prefer the castle to this place.' Having been found guilty of murder,

The prison courtyard, where felons would exercise daily.

Parker repeated his request for a cell in York Gaol, and as the law would not allow an insane person to suffer the death sentence, he got his wish, ending his days locked up and forgotten in a tiny cell.

In this new prison, separate areas were designated for men and women, the debtors were segregated and housed upstairs, while the other prisoners were detained on the ground floor below. Imprisonment for debt was very common. Before 1869, any debtor who did not qualify for bankruptcy proceedings could be imprisoned indefinitely by his or her creditor. They would only be released if they or a third party could pay off their debt, or in the unlikely event that their creditor relented or the debtor's insolvency could be proved to the court. Some debtors were released by acts of charity, but many died in custody.

In 1780, in a bid to ease overcrowding, the Female Prison was built adjacent to the Debtors' Prison. Though it was, as the name suggests, a designated female gaol, it also housed some male prisoners, as well as the new infirmary and chapel. The impressive façade of the Female Prison mirrored the architecture of the newly appointed County Court opposite,

The Female Prison at York.

which had been designed by John Carr and completed three years earlier, in 1777.

Mary Bateman, known as the 'Yorkshire Witch', was probably the most famous female to be executed at York. A criminal since childhood, Mary was forty-one years old when she was convicted of poisoning Rebecca Perigo in May 1808. Rebecca and her husband William, like many before them, had been duped by Bateman, who ran a fraudulent fortune-telling business under the name of 'Mrs Moore'. Thinking they had been put under a spell, the Perigos approached 'Moore' for assistance, and in the process of working her magic, Bateman used the opportunity to alleviate the Perigos of a great deal of money, before taking steps to silence them when they became suspicious of her credibility. After successfully murdering Mrs Perigo by feeding her pudding laced with poison, Bateman continued to leach money from her susceptible, grieving husband. However, once William Perigo's gullibility finally evaporated, Mary's time was up. In a sensational trial, during which her attempt to 'plead her belly' resulted in the judge ordering the courtroom doors to be barred, lest the co-opted jury of matrons tried to escape their duty, Mary was found guilty. Just three days after being convicted, Mary was hanged before a crowd of thousands, disappointing many who believed to the last that she would use her supernatural powers to escape the noose. The aura of her alleged

'pudding laced with poison'

mystic abilities must have lingered, however, as many of those paying to view her corpse parted with a further fee to purchase cured cuts of Mary's skin to use as a magic charm.

The Victorian Prison, the final chapter in York's gaols, is now lost to sight beneath the York Castle car park. One of the city's largest and most remarkable buildings, this new prison stood for less than a century before being entirely demolished. The Debtors' Prison and the Female Prison were closed toward the end of the nineteenth century, and the new Victorian Prison was built with the intention of coping with the rising number of felons. The build was of such a scale that it took ten years to complete, between 1825 and 1835. With four prison blocks radiating out from the central

The Victorian Prison building with radiating wings, adjacent to Clifford's Tower, top left corner, and Debtors' Prison, centre bottom. (Courtesy of York Museums Trust)

hub of the Governor's residence, like the spokes of an enormous wheel, it was surrounded by a huge, dark millstone perimeter wall, which encircled the entire castle site and cut the complex off from the rest of the city. The ancient North Gate was demolished and replaced with a new single gate to the north-west corner. The Victorian Prison only functioned as such until 1900, after which it was utilised as a military detention centre for a further thirty years or so, before finally being closed and demolished by the City Council in 1934.

Today, the former Debtors' Prison and the Female Prison, along with York Crown Court, complete three sides of the square facing Clifford's Tower in the former bailey of York Castle. Both the Debtors' Prison and the Female Prison were restored and converted into the York Castle Museum in 1938, and now the story of the prisons and the prisoners' pasts form part of an exhibition aptly housed within the former cells of the Debtors' Prison itself.

Policing York

York is one of only seven cities in the world whose cathedral boasts its own constabulary, and though the Minster Police may not be as well known as the Swiss Guard – the small force maintained by the Holy See at St Peter's Basilica in Rome, who are responsible for the safety of the Pope – St Peter's force has served the Minster and the Liberty for many hundreds of years.

Between 1285 and 1839, York Minster controlled its own Liberty – the walled area enclosing Minster Close, which grew to cover an area equating to about one third of the medieval city. Within the Liberty, the Dean and Chapter of York Minster held jurisdiction and appointed constables to maintain law and order. In fact, the Minster Police could well claim to be the oldest continuing police service in the county, possibly the world. Sir Robert Peel, acknowledged founder of the modern day police force, supposedly reviewed two policing bodies before he formed the Metropolitan Police Service in 1829; one being the Thames River Police and the other the Liberty of St Peter and Peter Prison constables, the latter being the Minster Police.

In 1839, control of the Liberty passed to the Corporation of York, with the Minster Police remaining closely linked with York City Police, who took over responsibility of policing the Liberty. Today, the small specialised constabulary consists of ten Minster Police officers, and while they are no longer attested (sworn in as constables), they instead utilise the 'any person' power of citizen's arrest, their modern day role to act as custodians of the Minster, as well as directing tourists and diligently holding 380 sets of keys!

With the rapid population growth in the nineteenth century (partly due to the influx of Irish immigrants fleeing the potato famine in the 1840s) the city authorities realised that the out-dated medieval system of constables was no longer effective in the face of the rising crime rate, and, in 1836, the first 'modern' police force was formed in York, replacing what had been termed as the 'Old Police', which was comprised of amateur/semi-professional parish constables and nightwatchmen.

As the need for policing grew, so did the need for police stations, and it was mooted that the police station at St Andrewgate, shared with the city's coal inspector, was no longer suitable, and new premises were acquired in May 1837. Cottages on Silver Street were leased from the City Commissioners at an annual rent of £22 and converted into York's new police station. Following this, Fulford Road station (now Copper's Lodge, a comfortable guest house) in Alma Grove, was acquired. Built in 1880 for the East Riding Constabulary, this solid red-brick building originally included a charge room and three cells, with the shed to the rear serving as the police stable.

Today, the Fulford Road police station, purpose-built in 1980, with twenty-two holding cells, provides the base for the city's police.

CHAPTER TWO

TRIAL & PUNISHMENT IN YORK

Justice for the City

As well as functioning as a gaol, York Castle was also the original seat of justice for the city. From the beginning of the fourteenth century, the Assize Courts for Yorkshire were based in the castle, and the prisoners who were awaiting trial were held in the castle's dungeons. Depending on the severity of the accusation, prisoners could spend some considerable time awaiting trial as the Assize Courts were normally held only twice a year, during Lent and summer. Judges rode on horseback from one county town to the next, trying all those charged with criminal offences too serious to be dealt with by the magistrates at the quarter sessions. Capital offences were heard at the Assize Courts – crimes ranging from murder, manslaughter and rape, as well as treason, major fraud or theft, arson, riot and rebellion. Guilt on any of these counts carried the death penalty prior to 1836, the year in which capital punishment was abolished for crimes other than murder and attempted murder.

The quarter sessions, as the name suggests, were county courts held by magistrates four times a year – Epiphany (January-March), Easter (April-June), Midsummer (July-September) and Michaelmas (October-December). These courts dealt with criminal matters from petty theft to rape, along with administrative matters such as licensing. Ranking lower still in the judicial system were the petty sessions; courts that met daily and formed the lowest tier in the English court system (known today as the Magistrates' Court). At the petty sessions, cases involving minor crimes were heard, such as charges of assault, petty theft and public drunkenness, along with licensing and civil matters such as claims of bastardy, child maintenance and adoption.

By 1777, however, cases could be heard in the newly appointed Assize Court building, the County Courthouse. Designed by John Carr to replace

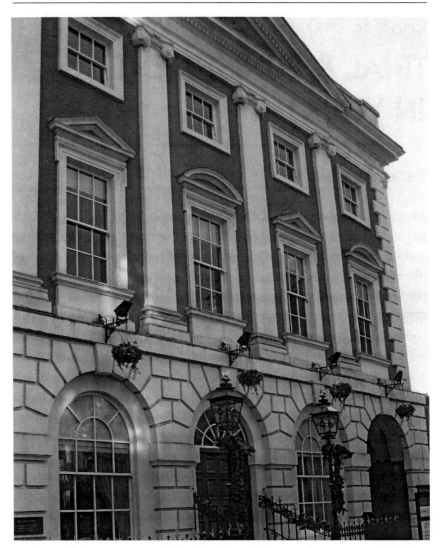

York's Guildhall.

the old Grand Jury House, the courthouse still houses York Crown Court today. With the addition of the Female Prison built in 1780 (positioned to the left of, and originally intended as an extension to, the new County Prison) these judicial edifices form three sides of the square facing Clifford's Tower in the former bailey of York Castle. Positioned around a circular lawn, this became known as the 'Eye of the Ridings', or the 'Eye of York', and

Carr's County Courthouse, now York Crown Court.

continues the tradition of York Castle as a site of justice and incarceration for nearly 1,000 years.

Public Punishments in York

Those convicted of crimes that carried the death penalty were invariably hanged at the gallows, and in high profile cases the body was often gibbeted. A common punishment, gibbeting could be imposed by a judge in addition to the sentence of execution, and was most often reserved for murderers, highwaymen, traitors, pirates and sheep stealers. Gibbets were often sited close to the place where the crime had been committed or next to a public highway (usually at a crossroads) and intended to discourage others from committing a similar offence. In some instances, the gibbeted bodies were displayed for years, as was the case of Francis Fearn, who was executed on the York Knavesmire gallows on Tuesday, 23 July 1782 for murdering a 'respectable watchmaker'. His body was hung in chains on Loxley Common, only being taken down by Mr Payne of Loxley, 'On whose land it stood, in the year 1807, having remained there twenty-five years.'

Another gruesome gibbeting legacy was uncovered some fifty years after the event, when a quantity of human bones, the 'shattered fragments' of three condemned murderers hanged at the York Tyburn on 28 July 1623, were unearthed from under the site of the gibbet, where their bodies had been displayed for 'a considerable time'. The bodies of the two executed men had been hung up at the roadside, close to where the guilty party had drowned their victim between Easingwold and Raskelf (and still marked on Ordnance Survey maps to this day as 'Gibbet Hill'), the third, perhaps by virtue of her sex, was buried beneath the gibbet.

Gibbet Hill, between Easingwold and Raskelf.

In 1677, John Webster, a well-known puritan writer, who was eyewitness to the confessions of the Easingwold trio and their resulting execution, recounted the events:

About the year of our Lord 1623 or 24 one Fletcher of Rascal, a Town in the North Riding of Yorkshire near unto the Forest of Gantress, a Yeoman of good Estate, did marry a young lusty Woman of Thornton Brigs, who had been formerly kind with one Ralph Raynard, who kept an Inn within half a mile from Rascall in the high road way betwixt York and Thuske, his Sister living with him.

This Raynard continued in unlawful lust with the said Fletchers Wife, who not content therewith conspired the death of Fletcher, one Mark Dunn being made privy and hired to assist in the murder. Which Raynard and Dunn accomplished upon the May-day by drowning Fletcher, as they came all three together from a Town called Huby, and acquainting the wife with the deed she gave them a Sack therein to convey his body, which they did and buried it in Raynards backyard or Croft where an old Oak-root had been stubbed up, and sowed Mustard-seed upon the place thereby to hide it. So they continued their wicked course of lust and drunkenness, and the neighbours did much wonder at Fletchers absence, but his wife did excuse it, and said that he was but gone aside for fear of some Writs being served upon him.

And so it continued until about the seventh day of July, when Raynard going to Toplifife Fair, and setting up his Horse in the Stable, the spirit of Fletcher in his usual shape and habit did appear unto him Oh Ralph repent repent for my revenge is at hand; and ever after until he was put in the Goal [sic] it seemed to stand before him, whereby he became sad and restless: And his own Sister overhearing his confession and relation of it to another person did through fear of losing her own life, immediately reveal it to Sir William Sheffield who lived at Rascall and was a Justice of Peace Whereupon they were all three apprehended and sent to the Gaol at York, where they were all three condemned and so executed accordingly near to the place where Raynard lived and where Fletcher was buried, the two men being hung up in irons, and the woman buried underneath the gallows.

York's Prestigious Execution Site

The area known as the 'Pavement' in front of All Saints' Church was the preserve of the higher-class execution by beheading; a fate that befell Thomas Percy, the 7th Earl of Northumberland, who was executed on a specially constructed scaffold here in 1572 for his part in the Northern Rebellion during the reign of Elizabeth I. Afterwards, his head was placed on Micklegate Bar, from whence it was recovered two years later by one of the Earl's sympathisers.

Dating to the twelfth century, Micklegate Bar is traditionally the gateway through which all reigning monarchs enter York, as well as being the prominent edifice upon which the severed heads of executed traitors were displayed. After the Yorkist defeat at the Battle of Wakefield in 1460, the victorious Lancastrians made a clear political statement when the head of Richard Plantagenet, 3rd Duke of York, was displayed on Micklegate wearing a mocking paper crown, along with the heads of the Earl of Salisbury and Plantagenet's son Edmund, the Earl of Rutland. However, the Duke's head only remained skewered on a pikestaff for three months, as in 1461, his son, King Edward IV, avenged his death by mirroring the enemy's grisly display and replaced the Yorkist heads with those of the Lancastrian leaders, who were captured at the Battle of Towton. As a preservative measure, heads were parboiled and seasoned with cumin to deter carrion birds from picking at the flesh, although the crows and magpies still made a fine feast of them.

Other heads of note to grace Micklegate Bar include those of Sir Henry 'Hotspur' Percy, displayed in 1403, and Sir William Plumpton, who happened to be on the wrong side at the wrong time during the Wars of the Roses and executed in 1405 on the orders of King Henry IV. The head of Lord Scrope was on view there in 1415, after his involvement in a plot to assassinate King Henry V. Many years later, in 1746, a brace of Jacobite heads, most notably those of William Conolly and James Mayne, were skewered there after the unsuccessful Jacobite Rebellion. Decapitated heads were clearly viewed as a long-term deterrent feature at the bar, as Mayne's head presumably would have remained in place longer had it not been 'illegally removed' after a nine-year stint, in 1754.

However, in deference to the severity of the crime, other lesser punishments were employed in cases of more minor offences; for example,

'prostitutes were branded on the face'

branding, an ancient punishment using red-hot irons, was not only painful but a lasting mark of humiliation and a sentence which was undertaken publicly. Vagabonds would be marked with the letter 'V', brawlers with the letter 'F' for 'fravmaker', while prostitutes were branded on the face making their re-entry into respectable society impossible. It was usual at the assizes and quarter sessions to order the accused to hold up their hands before sentence was passed, as previously branded prisoners physically held their own record of prior conviction.

In 1682, a case took place in York in which a couple slandered a young woman who they thought worthy of being branded a prostitute.

Stocks in the churchyard of the Priory Church of Holy Trinity, Micklegate.
(These stocks are a replica – the originals are incorporated into an exhibition on permanent display inside the church.)

This tiny street can be found between Colliergate and Fossgate, close to the Pavement.

The 'Cause Papers' for the diocesan courts of the Archbishop of York cites this case as one of defamation (sexual slander). Mary Spragg accused husband and wife, Robert and Catherine Crooke of calling her, 'A brasen faced whore and a painted whore ... and bid her looke in her forhead if she was not branded for a whore' – strong words indeed. Mary won her case.

Other penalties for petty criminals included flogging and whipping, and between Colliergate and Fossgate is the aptly named Whip-Ma-Whop-Ma-Gate Street (known in the sixteenth century as 'Whitnourwhatnourgate'), the shortest street in York with the longest name. The present street name evolved when the area was designated the site of the city's whipping post where public floggings took place. We know that in the first half of the seventeenth century in York, the going rate for the official carrying out this punishment was 4d. Being placed in the pillory or stocks was also an efficacious chastisement in which the crowd would readily participate – the former, a lockable wooden frame on a pole with holes for the person's head and hands, the latter, a version where the feet were held in place, both intended to subject the occupant to humiliation and ridicule, with spectators often throwing unpleasant objects of the rotten egg and old cabbage variety. On occasion however, the strength of public feeling could escalate to inflicting a serious pelting, with some unfortunates maimed for life or even dying in situ. Though their use went out of favour at the beginning of the nineteenth century, the pillory was not abolished in Britain until 1837, and use of the stocks was not abolished until 1872.

Humans weren't the only species to suffer a good whipping in York, however, as specific to the city was 'Whip Dog Day' which took place

A ducking stool, similar to the one found in York.

every St Luke's Day, on 18 October. It was said that a dog once got into the Minster and ate some consecrated wafer, so as a punishment to the entire canine fraternity, once a year local boys whipped all the dogs they could find in the city. This was probably the pretext for a control measure that was exercised in most other cities, where a once yearly communal dog-drive would rid the streets of the packs of wild roaming dogs which used to present a genuine problem.

York also boasted two ducking stools, one located in Blue Bridge Lane and another in the garden of one of the cottages on Postern Lane, where a pool of stagnant water was employed for this once very popular method of punishment. Reserved for females who, '... used fake measures or brewed bad beer', as well as gossiping women who could not hold their tongue and were regarded as a public nuisance. When sentencing a woman to the ducking stool, magistrates would determine the number of 'duckings' she should suffer. In some instances a 'get out' clause would be applied, as in

The scold's bridle. (Courtesy of Mary Evans Picture Library)

the case of Margery Watson in 1657, a notorious scold who was sentenced to ducking unless she apologised to the wife of James Wilkinson within one month either in church or even more publicly at the market cross. Gossiping was also a transgression punishable with the scold's bridle, a metal frame placed over the woman's head with a bit pressed into the mouth to prevent speech; the last recorded use of the scold's bridle in Britain was in 1824.

Punishment in the form of public humiliation was certainly thought to be most efficacious, and a further example of which was the drunkard's cloak. An individual found guilty of committing a petty crime, such as public drunkenness, would be forced to walk through the streets wearing

a barrel as a demeaning chastisement. More extreme on the
punishment scale were mutila-
tions, which were a brutal but
common penalty for stealing
or poaching; the cutting off
of hands, clipping of ears or
the slitting of noses were all
employed. All of these punishments, along with executions
by pressing, burning, beheading
and hanging, were all carried
out publicly.

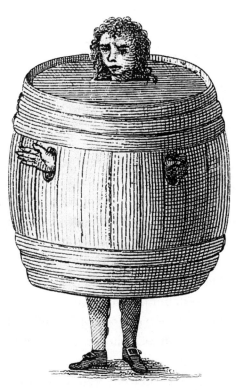

Drunkard's cloak. (Courtesy of Mary Evans
Picture Library)

CHAPTER THREE

GALLOWS GALORE!

Execution Sites Around the City of York

It naturally follows that those found guilty of criminal transgression needed to be punished under the law, and the severity of the punishment handed down was often cruelly tailored to reflect the crime that had been committed. Thieves might have their hands cut off, spies may have had their eyes put out, petty criminals might be put in the pillory, whipped or branded, but for those found guilty of a capital offence this carried the ultimate sentence of death. And to act as a deterrent to any would-be criminals, these sentences were carried out in public.

Although records indicate that York's Holy Trinity Priory had its own set of gallows in the city from very early on, these were eventually removed in the mid-1100s, when King Stephen gave away the site on which they stood in order for St James' Chapel to be built. The chapel served as a place of burial for convicted felons up until the sixteenth century, although at least one post-execution interment didn't take place – a pardon was issued in 1280 to a man who miraculously came back to life after being hanged while on his way to be buried!

Both St Mary's Abbey and York Minster exercised control over all that went on within their own walled boundaries, along with boasting their own gaols and gallows. Until 1379, the gallows in the Liberty of St Mary's Abbey was used for the execution of capital offenders. However, as a consequence of a dispute that erupted with the abbey monks, it was decided that a municipal gallows should be erected. The chosen place was originally the site of a gibbet post that had stood on the west side of Knavesmire – a large open space outside of the city walls that today faces onto the Tadcaster Road opposite Pulleyn Drive, and falls within the boundary of York Racecourse. The notorious York Tyburn, or the 'Three Legged Mare' as it

Site of the York Tyburn on the Knavesmire, overlooking what is now York Racecourse.

was also known, was an expediently designed tripod arrangement which facilitated multiple executions of felons. The condemned would be taken from York Prison in an open cart, sat on their coffin and already wearing their shroud, jolted on out through Micklegate Bar towards the Knavesmire for their public execution. Executions were carried out on this spot between 1379 and 1801 and it is now marked with an informative plaque.

The gallows at the Knavesmire were not unique within York, however. As mentioned earlier, St Mary's Abbey possessed its own gallows, which were located in the aptly named Gallows Close on Burton Stone Lane, while another gallows, under the control of the Dean and Chapter of York Minster, was sited in Horsefair, today situated at the junction of Haxby and Wiggington roads to the north of the city. The Church was clearly a heavy hitter in the capital punishment stakes as the Archbishop of York also had gallows in Fossgate. Closely associated with the Minster, St Leonard's Hospital governed the gallows at Garrow Hill in Green Dyke Lane, the present

Thief Lane being the route taken by condemned prisoners. The gallows at St Leonard's was kept busy with recorded executions from 1374, and while there was an interruption in use, a period in the mid-sixteenth century probably attributable to the Reformation, the Garrow Hill gallows were back in business again by 1571 and used until 1676, finally being dismantled in June 1700. With the majority of executions at this point being carried out at the Knavesmire most of the other gallows had fallen into disuse too.

Although the public nature of such spectacles was supposed to act as a deterrent to the populace, public hangings were often viewed as a form of mass entertainment, with an atmosphere of something perhaps akin to an open-air concert of today. Crowds, including families with young children, would take a picnic and make a day of it, and making the most of the York Tyburn's proximity to the racecourse, bookmakers would happily take bets on the time it took the convicted to die on the gallows as well as wagers on the runners and riders.

The first execution to take place at the new Knavesmire gallows was that of Edward Hewison on 31 March 1379. A native of Stockton, Hewison was a private soldier in the Earl of Northumberland's Light Horse Brigade, and was tried and convicted at the Spring Assizes for raping twenty-two-year-old serving girl Louise Bentley. Justice was reasonably swift in this instance, as Hewison had committed the crime on 28 February, not long before the first of the twice-yearly assizes (he would otherwise have languished in York Castle until the case could be heard at the Summer Assizes). As this was the first execution at the new gallows, Hewison's demise proved something of a celebrity hanging, drawing crowds from the neighbouring towns and villages as well as numerous spectators from the city itself. The body was hung from a gibbet three miles from the girl's home town of Sheriff Hutton.

In the intervening period between this first execution and the last to take place on the Knavesmire in 1801 (coincidentally the last person hanged at the York Tyburn was also a private soldier and he too was found guilty of rape – Edward Hughes was hanged on 29 August 1801), many felons, both infamous and forgotten, swung from the 'Three Legged Mare', the memory of which lives on in the name of a popular pub in High Petergate, and in keeping with the theme of aptly named public houses, this street is also home to the Last Drop Inn.

Despite the obvious taste and enthusiasm for the spectacle of public execution, the ultimate decision to move the proceedings to York Castle Gaol was probably heavily influenced by the objectionable first impression of the city given by the Knavesmire gallows, as they were located next to one of the main highways into York. The gallows were also a cause of major road congestion. In an article printed on 25 July 1800, the *York Herald* explained, 'Thus will be removed from one of the principal roads leading to the city that disagreeable nuisance, the gallows; and thus will the inhabitants and passengers be no longer interrupted, and their humanity hurt, by the leading of unfortunate people to the place of execution.' As a consequence, it was decided at a civic meeting that investment in a new gallows should be made, in order that the, 'Entrance to the town should no longer be annoyed by dragging criminals through the streets'. Though sensibility won on this day, the Knavesmire gallows stood (albeit unused) for a further eleven years before it was finally dismantled in 1812.

The Three-Legged Mare, High Petergate.   The Last Drop Inn, High Petergate.

The 'New Drop', as it became known, was constructed by Joseph Halfpenny, a joiner from Blake Street in York, and was set up at the back of the castle in an area boarded by the Castle Mills Bridge and the River Ouse, roughly where the roundabout by St George's car park is today. Looking toward York Castle Museum, there is a small doorway in the wall to the right, through which the condemned prisoners were led. Completed on 8 March 1801, the first executions were not to take place until Saturday, 28 August 1802, when James Roberts, William Barker and William Jackson were all hanged there. Roberts had been found guilty of stealing nineteen sheep, Barker for stealing three horses and Jackson for the robbery of a Mr Wetherhead of Malton. The new gallows at the castle continued as York's principal place of execution until the 1820s, when it was superseded by a structure variously described as, 'the New Drop in front of St George's fields'. This new gallows was trundled out into the open area in front of the Debtors' Prison, all the better to facilitate the multitude of spectators who would crowd to watch an execution.

It was usual for prisoners condemned at the previous assizes to await the next scheduled day of execution and then be hanged in groups, irrespective of gender. Up until 1830, Monday was the designated day for murderers to be hanged, while the execution of other criminals was kept back for Saturdays as this allowed for the largest weekend crowds – until 29 May 1868 that is, as this was the date Parliament passed the Capital Punishment (Amendment) Act ending all public hangings. The last public execution in York was that of Frederick Parker on Saturday, 4 April 1868, for the murder of Daniel Driscoll on 29 February that same year. The two had met on release from the Beverley House of Correction and it seemed that Driscoll was rather better set than Parker, with £4 11s in his pocket and a silver watch and chain. It was for

Execution day at York, c. 1820. Thomas Rowlandson. (Courtesy of York Museums Trust, York Art Gallery)

his effects that Parker murdered the unfortunate man, before dumping his body in a ditch. On the day of his execution, shortly after noon, Parker shook hands with the governor, under-governor and head warders on the scaffold, wishing them 'Goodbye' and hoping they might meet in heaven. After kneeling in prayer the last public spectacle of execution was brought to a close. From that day forth, private executions were carried out on a balcony style gallows built at the end of one of the wings of the Debtors' Prison, although members of the press were still admitted to witness executions at this time.

A Big Draw

At the time when York's public hangings took place in the capacious open area in St George's Fields, special trains were being laid on to better facilitate transport of the immense crowds drawn to the executions. However, the majority of spectators who came to watch the execution of James Waller at noon on Saturday, 4 January 1862 came on foot. Many had set off in the early hours of the morning from the West Riding (from whence Waller hailed), and it was noted that those who were fatigued by their long nocturnal walk took respite by sleeping in the field opposite the drop, while others perched themselves on the rails surrounding St George's Field in an 'easy jaunty manner'. Clearly the deterrent that such public spectacles should have occassioned was absent, as demonstrated by the 'ribald and disgusting expressions which came from others in reference to the unfortunate man's approaching end', leaving one observer at a loss 'to find the working of that great moral lesson which the public strangling of a criminal was designed to effect.' Incidentally, the headcount for this particular execution was put at between eight to ten thousand people – Waller was thirty-one years of age at the time of his execution, and had been found guilty of the wilful murder of William Smith, a gamekeeper, the previous November.

Special note was always made of any execution where the strength of the crowd was considered to be great, usually referred to in the records as 'a large concourse of spectators' and this proved to be the case with the considerable number of people who came to witness the hanging of

George and Maria Merrington on Tuesday, 13 April 1649. The execution of the couple took place at the St Leonard's gallows and proved to be a great attraction. The murderous pair had killed William Rex a little over a month before on 9 March, before concealing the body in a shallow grave in their kitchen. They were taken to the execution site in a cart from York Castle at 7.30 a.m., guarded by the Sheriff's officers and a troop of dragoons. The magnitude of people clearly caused a great difficulty in negotiating the castle gate, owing to the, '... great multitude of people with whom that street was crowded from top to bottom, so that nothing could be seen but a forest of hats', though by all accounts this 'forest of hats' was removed as a mark of respect as the condemned couple passed by. However, as the pair progressed to the gallows, Fossgate became so crowded that one woman had her leg broken in the crush and another young man broke his thigh bone. The crowds persisted into Walmgate bar, where the cart was forced to halt because the Merringtons had

'one woman had her leg broken in the crush'

fainted, however, revived by a glass of mint water supplied by the obliging landlady of the Golden Barrel, followed by a glass of wine each, they were taken on to the gallows at 9.20 a.m. and were subsequently hanged before 'thousands of spectators'.

We can only speculate as to why the demise of certain criminals drew more of a crowd on some occasions than others – sometimes the notoriety of the crime committed affected the draw, or even something as simple as the weather. The executions, in August 1537, of Sir Robert Aske and Lord Hussey for their involvement in the Pilgrimage of Grace, a religious insurrection led against Henry VIII, drew what was described as a 'large concourse' and a 'large number' of spectators, while it was estimated that on 28 March 1587 some 8,000 people witnessed the hanging of Frederick de Alcyonius, Richard de Aldrich and William de Malcolm, who had been found guilty of 'petty treason'. (Unfortunately, there are no surviving records of the North-Eastern Assize circuit for the Tudor period, so we do not know what their crime was, although petty treason or 'petit treason' was an offence under common law which involved the betrayal of a superior by a subordinate, for example the murder of a master by his servant). Whatever their crime, the full penalty of the law was carried out and after the execution all three were beheaded and quartered, with their heads being displayed at Micklegate Bar.

There was, however, another post-execution option available for the disposal of the deceased's body, and that was for the corpse to be given over to surgeons to be 'dissected and anatomized' – a practice which was formerly prohibited by the Roman Church but was once again permitted after the Reformation. As medical research grew so too did the need for cadavers, and in England, by the 1700s, the bodies of executed criminals and the 'unclaimed poor' were given over to feed the increasing need. Sentence of dissection also afforded an additional deterrent aspect as the prospect of being given over to the anatomists for bodily desecration after death was, to most, as horrific to contemplate if not more so than actually being hanged. Indeed, in some cases public feeling against the practice was so strong that bodies were frequently 'saved' from the surgeon's table by a surge of angry crowds intent on snatching the body away post execution, ensuring an intact Christian burial.

However, this was a sentiment far from the mind of Ebenezer Wright who, before he was hanged on Saturday, 30 March 1833 for arson, had kept the body of his late wife hidden under their bed for two days before selling her to the anatomists in order to save on funeral costs! Wright, along with his accomplice Norburn, was found guilty of firing a stack of straw and hay after both parties turned King's evidence against each other (Wright harbouring a suspicion that Norton was conducting an extramarital affair with Mrs Wright). Subsequently, both were tried and convicted on their own evidence; Norburn assisting Wright in his revenge attack against a Mr Oxley, a solicitor who had previously brought a case of assault against Wright. Norton latterly received a reprieve, but Wright, perhaps in fateful retribution for the callous treatment of his wife's corpse, made up the triple execution – also executed were one Thomas Law, convicted of aggravated highway robbery, and Mary Hunter – which drew an estimated crowd of 4,000 to 5,000 on that day.

A Terminal Profession – York's Celebrity Hangmen

In York the position of hangman was usually filled by a convicted felon who had been pardoned sentence of death on the condition that he accepted the job. This was the case with Thomas Hadfield, who gained notoriety as the hangman who officiated at the flamboyant execution of Dick Turpin – rather ironically, Hadfield himself had been reprieved from sentence of death having been found guilty of highway robbery.

However, York's most infamous hangman must have been the twice sentenced, twice reprieved William 'Mutton' Curry. A convicted sheep-stealer, hence the ovine sobriquet, Curry's repeated sentence of death had been commuted twice to transportation and in 1802, while being held in York Castle awaiting his enforced passage to Australia, he was prevailed upon to accept the vacant position of hangman. Curry was known to be partial to a drop of gin (hardly surprising given the nature of his forced employ) and this consequently led to some less than professional executions. On one occasion, Curry was so drunk *The Times* reported that, 'The executioner, in a bungling manner and with great difficulty (being in a state of intoxication), placed the cap over the culprit's face and attempted several times to place the rope round his neck, but was unable.' It took the assistance of the gaoler and the sheriff's officers to complete the job before the incensed and increasingly hostile crowd, who ended up demanding Curry's own execution. Another time, clearly the worse for drink, Curry actually ended up falling through the trap door himself!

Between April 1853 and August 1856 there were no executions at York, however, a new executioner had to be found in order to hang twenty-eight-year-old William Dove who, after six attempts of administering strychnine, had finally succeeded in murdering his wife. On Saturday, 9 August 1856, an estimated 15,000 to 20,000 strong throng of spectators witnessed Thomas Askern, imprisoned for debt, carry out his duty as the new hangman. Askern held the position until 1868, performing the last public execution, that of Frederick Parker. While Askern was said to be the last hangman to hold a provincial post anywhere in Britain, this did not detract from the fact that he was incompetent at his job, botching many executions and leaving many of his unfortunate 'clients' to dangle at the end of the rope suffering unnecessarily.

Transportation: An Enlightened Alternative to Execution

For those lucky enough not to receive the death penalty, transportation was an alternative punishment for both major and petty crimes, and was exercised in Great Britain and Ireland from the 1620s until well into the 1800s. Those sentenced at quarter sessions held elsewhere in Yorkshire would be detained along with those who were likewise sentenced at the York County Assizes, remaining in York Gaol while awaiting shipment.

The Transportation Act of 1717 made transportation to America the punishment for serious crimes and continued until 1776, when the Declaration of Independence made transportation to the American colonies no longer viable. However, even following the American Revolution sentence of transportation was still handed down, with male felons being held on prison ships, or prison hulks, permanently moored off the south coast of England (the preference being to hold female prisoners in local gaols). Forced to look elsewhere, the British Government opted to utilise the newly claimed colonies in Australia and from

The Half Moon Court in the County Gaol, where criminals awaiting transportation took their exercise – their graffiti can still be seen.

An example of a prisoner's graffiti from the County Gaol.

1787 the new territory provided a penal repository for those sentenced to seven years or longer.

Later in the Victorian period, transportation was replaced with penal servitude, a term of imprisonment that usually included hard labour and was served on native soil, and ranged from a term of three years to life. After the 1853 Penal Servitude Act was passed, only long-term transportation was retained, and the sentence of transportation was finally abolished in 1857.

CHAPTER FOUR

ARSONISTS

English law terms arson as a common law offence dealing with the criminal destruction of buildings by fire, typically the crime of maliciously, voluntarily, and wilfully setting fire to the building, buildings, or other property of another or of burning one's own property for an improper purpose; such as to collect insurance.

Probably the most notable incidence of arson in York was the blaze that devastated York Minster, which took hold in the early hours of Monday, 9 July 1984. While the cause of the fire has never been conclusively proven, it was attributed by some as 'divine retribution' in the light of the appointment of controversial clergyman the Right Revered David Jenkins as Bishop of Durham – UFO involvement was even suggested! However, the Yorkshire Fire Brigade concluded that rather than being divinely directed or influenced by extra terrestrials, the most likely cause of the fire was a lightning strike shortly after midnight, probably due to the sultry weather the region was experiencing. However, this was not the first time York Minster had been ravaged by fire.

In 1068, two years after the Norman Conquest, the good people of York rebelled against the new regime. While the uprising was initially effective, on the arrival of William the Conqueror the rebellion was severely quashed, and the city was ravaged as part of his 'harrying of the North', with the first stone minster badly damaged by fire.

Construction of a new minster was undertaken by Archbishop Thomas in around 1080 and it was this cathedral that was to become the York Minster we know today; the Norman origins of which were once more revealed after the minster was again seriously damaged by fire, but this time by deliberate arson in 1829.

On Sunday, 1 February 1829, Jonathan Martin was among those attending evensong at the minster. Martin was the product of an unsettled and staunch upbringing; emotional trauma experienced in his early life, combined with a probable skull fracture sustained at the age of twenty-one when he was attempting to desert the navy after having been press-ganged, makes it possible that Martin suffered some mental instability. On that February evening he initially became agitated by what he thought was a buzzing sound coming from the organ. After service was over he hid in the church by concealing himself behind one of the monuments, emerging afterward into the minster's empty darkness. Martin then proceeded to stack prayer books and cushions and set them on fire, in turn igniting the woodwork in the choir, before promptly escaping through a window.

Around 6 a.m. the following morning, choristers on their way across the yard saw sparks rising from the cathedral roof and as they got closer they noticed that the frost on the ground had melted. On feeling the heat radiating from the stone work and seeing the glow emitting from inside, they ran to raise the alarm. By 7 a.m. church bells all over the city were ringing out to summon additional firefighting assistance, and even though fire engines were in early attendance the cathedral roof was beyond saving. Limited firefighting capabilities and the ferocity of the blaze forced the evacuation of those fighting the fire, as the melting lead from the roof poured from the mouths of the gargoyle water spouts, the supporting limestone pillars cracked, and shortly before noon, the first cross-beam fell from the roof with the others collapsing in quick succession. (The minster's nave is the widest in England, and the over-ambitious span of the Norman columns proved too great to be vaulted in stone and so it was roofed in wood – a marvel of medieval engineering but susceptible to combustion.)

Though the choir was entirely destroyed and filled with blazing timbers, it was now at least possible to contain the fire, although it was after midnight before the blaze was finally extinguished. The minster was filled with scorched rubble and the floor of the choir partly collapsed. The Clerk of Works, John Browne, when directing the clean-up operation, discovered that the columns of the nave extended far beneath the collapsed floor. Further excavation and investigation revealed the true extent of the Norman crypt, the undercroft, which today houses the minster's museum.

In the aftermath of the fire, attention turned to cause and apportioning blame – the contents of a series of what were initially taken as anonymous

An illustration of York Minster after the fire. (Courtesy of York Museums Trust, York Art Gallery)

letters received over the previous year warning of divine judgment on all clergy now seemed to point strongly to the possibility of arson. Closer inspection of the crazed correspondence revealed the letters were signed with the initials 'JM' and included an address!

The authorities wasted no time in calling at No. 60 Aldwark, Jonathan Martin's home in the city, but having fled the scene immediately after setting the blaze he was not at home. When questioned, the neighbours' statements proved rather enlightening as they described someone who seemed to be obsessed with divine retribution. Further investigation confirmed that Martin had previously escaped from the Gateshead Asylum, where he was being held for threatening to shoot the Bishop of Oxford.

An immediate warrant for Martin's arrest was issued, and on 5 February he was apprehended near his family home near Hexham, and made no attempt to resist being held or to protest his innocence, instead stating that he had been carrying out God's will.

It was clear that Martin was 'mentally disturbed', though whether his upbringing and early experiences had any bearing on his mental condition we can only surmise. By any standards Martin's family were unusual. Jonathan was one of twelve siblings, his father, Fenwick Martin, was a fencing instructor while his mother Isabella seems to have been responsible for instilling religious fervour. One younger brother, John, became a famous painter, while the elder brother, William, dedicated twenty years of his life to the development of a perpetual motion machine. Jonathan seems to have been profoundly affected by his mother's strictures concerning hell, and from the age of eight he experienced visions and was convinced that thunderstorms were a divine punishment for his own unconscious sins.

After witnessing the murder of his sister by a neighbour at a young age, and being press-ganged into the navy for six years (sustaining a serious blow to the head as previously mentioned), Martin became a Wesleyan preacher in 1814, but his views proved too strong. As a non-conformist he believed all prayer should come from the heart rather than recited from formal liturgy, and published pamphlets condemning the clergy as 'Vipers of Hell'. Martin was eventually committed to the West Auckland Lunatic Asylum for the threatened assassination of the Bishop of Oxford, before his transfer and escape from the Gateshead Asylum.

Martin was committed for trial in York on 31 March 1829. His defence was conducted at his artist brother John's expense by Henry Brougham, who had gained some measure of notoriety in defending Queen Caroline in the divorce proceedings instigated by her husband George IV. The money spent on legal costs was wasted as Jonathan simply agreed with everything the prosecution put forward, while apparently smiling a great deal. In a courtroom so full that even the lawyers were not always able to find a seat, a detachment of yeomanry were present throughout the trial as the vehemence of public feeling against Martin ran so high there were concerns the accused might be lynched.

Portrait of Jonathan Martin by Edward Lindley. (Courtesy of York Museums Trust, York Art Gallery)

On 2 April, the presiding judge declared Martin not guilty on the grounds of insanity; it had taken the jury just seven minutes to decide that his actions were those of one of unsound mind, much to the dissatisfaction of the baying public gallery. Martin was sent to the Bethlehem Royal Hospital – 'Bedlam' – for the rest of his life, dying nine years later, on 26 May 1838, aged fifty-six.

York Minster was fully restored within three years of Martin's arson, although the minster did suffer a further major fire in 1840, when a careless workman left a candle lit while working in the south-west tower.

Female Fire Starters

Saturday, 30 April 1649 saw the execution of two convicted female arsonists, hanged with fourteen men and five other women, all of whom had been found guilty at the Lent Assizes that year – their crimes ranging from rebellion, infanticide, attempted murder and murder by crucifixion!

Twenty-nine-year-old Grace Bland had set fire to her mistress's house in Clifton on the outskirts of the city and burnt it to the ground. Clearly an ill-fated property as it was in this same house where two years previously the Drysdale sisters had poisoned their sweethearts with drinks laced with oxalic acid.

In company on the gallows with Grace that morning was twenty-eight-year-old Ellen Nicholson, who had been found guilty of wilfully setting fire to her master's house and destroying all the furniture and belongings contained therein, as well as the adjoining outbuildings, four horses, three cows, two calves, three stacks of wheat, two of barley, four of hay and two of straw.

This multiple execution of twenty-one felons necessitated two sledges to transport seven men apiece and two carts for the condemned women. A strong guard of fifty-four dragoons and Sheriff's officers accompanied the prisoners on their last journey, but on entering Castlegate they were forced to stop for some time in view of the mass of people who had gathered to watch. Joining in one voice to sing psalms on their way to execution, arriving at the Tyburn at 10.10 a.m., within five minutes 'twenty-one lifeless corpses were hanging suspended between heaven and earth', witnessed by thousands.

A fire set with deliberate intent starts with the first malicious ignition – no matter how small.

'A very large concourse of people' were also assembled to see twenty-four-year-old Robert Driffield and twenty-two-year-old Mark Edmund hanged at the Tyburn on Wednesday, 2 August 1672. Both men were found guilty of setting fire to six corn stacks, the property of Mr George Robinson at Skelton, just on the outskirts of York. This arson had been committed on the Mayday of that year, one of the few public holidays enjoyed by the working classes in the seventeenth century. Both bodies were buried in the churchyard of St Mary's, Bishophill Senior, which, though sadly demolished in 1963, was itself one of the oldest churches in York and retaining the only church tower in the city not to have been consumed by the conflagration of the Conqueror's repression of 1068 mentioned earlier.

However, probably the biggest draw for the execution of a convicted arsonist was on Tuesday, 2 April 1628, when an estimated 8,000 to 9,000 strong crowd turned out to see Robert Storie hanged at the Knavesmire. A native of Clifton, Stone had been found guilty of burning down the dwelling house and out buildings of a Mr R. Wilson in the January of that year. We know nothing of Storie's motives, just that 'the culprit died very hardly' and in this instance escaped the anatomists' clutches, as his body was buried in the churchyard of St Mary's Abbey.

Although her hand was not the one that lit the flame, mother of nine Mary Hunter professed her innocence of indirect arson, right up to the very point that the drop fell on Saturday, 30 March 1833. She was insistent to the last that she was not guilty of bribery and threats against her serving maid Hannah Gray. Described as a 'simple country girl', Hannah had set fire to three stacks of wheat at the coercion of her mistress. Clearly manipulating Hannah, who was born with developmental disabilities, Mary Hunter had promised the girl, 'A new frock if she did it, and that if she did not she would tear her liver out, and that if she told anybody she would tear her to pieces.' And so ended the life of Mary Hunter at age forty-seven, before an estimated crowd of 4,000 to 5,000 people – all for the sake of avenging a grudge against a neighbour, who refused to pay 4*d* for the use of the Hunter's pinfold to hold his foals.

Never a 'dying' trade – the temporary occupiers of the condemned cell kept York's coffin makers busy.

Though never carried out, an ultimatum was issued and a serious threat of arson made against the Lord Mayor of York in 1777, which was provoked by the fear of the imminent arrival of the press gangs coming to force the men of York to join the military. Anyone between the ages of eighteen and fifty-five were viable 'volunteers' and were signed up for years at a time against their will, with men outside of the specified age range often taken as well. The citizens of York were so incensed that the Lord Mayor had sanctioned their coming to the city that there was a minor uprising on 26 January 1777. The mayor was sent an anonymous letter threatening to burn down both his house and the Mansion House if any man were taken from York by the press gangs. Although the City Corporation offered 100 guineas reward for the identity of the sender, no information was ever forthcoming.

CHAPTER FIVE
COUNTERFEITERS & COINERS

Ever since the advent of the circulation of coins as currency people have been tempted to 'adjust' their value in their pecuniary favour. The milled edge of a modern English pound coin is engraved with the words *decus et tutamen*, the term meaning 'an ornament and safeguard'. Originally, these words were stamped around the edge of

A King Charles II sovereign.

coins to indicate whether it had been tampered with in an offence known as 'clipping'. The shavings of the precious metal were harvested, along with the metallic dust collected in another method of debasing coinage called 'sweating', where coins would be placed in a bag and vigorously shaken, producing precious dust that could then be collected.

All sorts of people were involved with coining, from children who might be used to deliver bags of clippings, to innkeepers who would rent out rooms for people to clip coins in. Some shopkeepers would even lend out their takings for a small fee to coiners who would clip them and then return them back to the shopkeeper for re-circulation. Of course counterfeit coins were far more difficult to spot then than in today's currency, as the light-weight, thin and poor quality coins made it difficult to tell if they had been falsified or tampered with.

The constant shortage of currency also helped create a steady market for counterfeit coins, a circumstance which was viewed very seriously by the authorities as an excessive injection of false money into the economy would compete with the legitimate government input of coinage.

essentially jeopardising the state of trade or even bringing it to a standstill. As a result, 'coining' was classed as treason and merited punishment by death.

Of course the introduction of paper money presented forgers with a further opportunity to counterfeit currency. Before the Bank Charter Act of 1844 tying the sole issue of bank notes to the Bank of England, private banks had the right to issue their own notes, thus broadening the scope for forgery and fraud.

In legal terms 'uttering' a false or bad note was the act of passing such and also applied to counterfeit coinage. All transgressions fell under the Forgery Act and were punishable by death, until two years after the consolidation of the Act in 1830 when the death penalty was abolished for most of the offences, and for all remaining offences in 1837.

Fiscal Felons

Before this time, however, those convicted of forgery, uttering, counterfeiting or coining were all liable to be hanged for their crimes, and this was the fate that befell Frederick Gottfried and Thomas Conrat on Friday, 27 March 1575, for 'coining guineas in the Thursday Market, in the city of York.'

The street running to the south east of what was the Thursday Market is Jubbergate. It was here that in 1585 another pair of coiners, George de Kirwan, aged thirty-four, and Thomas de Alasco, aged thirty-nine, were

'liable to be hanged for their crimes'

arrested for coining guineas at the house of Simon Pontius, a silversmith of York who was presumably in possession of some useful metallurgical working equipment. As was custom, they were drawn to their execution at the Tyburn on sledges and were apparently resigned to their fate and died penitent. They were both were buried at St Helen's, Fishergate, located in what is now Winterscale Street, and possibly amongst the last burials to take place there as it had fallen into disuse by the late fifteenth century, the parish being amalgamated with that of St Lawrence in 1586.

The Thursday Market – the site is now occupied by St Sampson's Square.

Multiple coiners were executed on Tuesday, 6 April 1604, at the Tyburn, for, 'coining and paying money, well knowing it to be counterfeit and bad.' The hanging of Richard Cullingworth aged forty-three, Elizabeth Bradwith aged thirty, Hannah Bulmer aged twenty-eight and Jane Buckel aged thirty-four, all of whom were from Walmgate in the city, was apparently witnessed by a 'large concourse of spectators.'

The neighbourhood of Walmgate was home to the bulk of the poorer classes of York, a district where those at the bottom of the social scale were tightly packed in filthy, diseased conditions, and human waste was left to accumulate in the alleys until there was enough to be collected and added to huge dung hills like the one behind St Margaret's Church in Walmgate. Small wonder then that they, and many others like them, felt forced by circumstance to succumb to the temptation that counterfeit coinage might afford them.

Edward Wells, a forty-year-old bricklayer from Northallerton, was found guilty of forging and publishing a counterfeit promissory note (a written promise to repay a loan or debt under specific terms) in 1753, with the intent of defrauding one William Horseman. He put on quite a show of bravado on the day of his execution, on Monday 28 April. Standing on the gallows he removed his hat, wig and handkerchief, unbuttoned his shirt and then, opening the noose, he kissed the rope before putting it under his chin. When the time came and the cart was drawn away, Wells threw himself off 'with the greatest resolution'. Executed along with Wells on that day was seventeen-year-old convicted murderer Bezaliel Knowles, who didn't make such a flamboyant end as Wells, though equally memorable in his falling over backwards into the cart before the executioner could fix

Various tools were employed in the business of 'coining' and none more so that a trusty pair of tin-snips.

the halter around his neck. He did, however, behave with much 'decency and contrition', and after ample confession he died penitent.

In 1773, the Government's determination to stamp out coining led to the passing of The Coin Act, which rendered anyone in mere possession of a 'light guinea' guilty of the crime of coining. They were expected to give the counterfeit money up, in spite of the fact that they would receive no reimbursement and be left out of pocket. While organised coining groups did exist and operated on a productive scale, it was often the working classes and the poor who turned to coining to make a profit, with the meagre manufacture of just a single coin. However, the harsh reality of the Government's measures left many such needy individuals with worthless currency in their pockets.

Presumably, amongst the crowd who turned out to see William Waddington hang on the morning of Saturday, 12 April 1794 were some of those working and poor townsfolk whom he had previously swindled. A native of York, the apparently hitherto 'respectable' Waddington had been found guilty of counterfeiting coins of the realm '... and paying the same to diverse people in York.' In this instance, Waddington had forged coins by 'colouring', which is disguising a base metal with a gilded veneer to give the appearance of the real thing. Two methods of colouring were typically employed, either by 'fire gilding', where the base core coin was coated with a liquid gold/mercury amalgam and then heated to drive off the majority of the mercury, or by building up repeated layers of gold leaf. At forty-two years of age, Waddington left a wife and seven children who all visited him on the morning of his execution. After their parting, Waddington was said to have stated that the terrors of death were now over.

Bad Notes

One of the many private banks in existence in eighteenth-century York was Raper, Clough & Swann, which was ultimately absorbed by the Royal Bank of Scotland after several incarnations, but in 1806 the bank occupied 45 Coney Street. On Saturday, 5 April of that year George Ormond, a thirty-year-old butler, was hanged after being found guilty of forging one of Raper, Clough & Swann's bank notes. Executed at the New Drop, Ormond declared

A hefty bolt held the door of the condemned cell closed.

that the forgery was the only crime that he had ever perpetrated. This had no bearing on his ultimate fate however.

The first of only two executions that were ever to take place at the under-utilised gallows of the city gaol at Bishophill was that of forger David Anderson, who on Saturday, 20 August 1809 was hanged for 'uttering bad notes'. Arrested at the house of Robert Dentis, a flour-dealer who operated out of Low Ousegate in the city, Anderson was betrayed by Dentis, who gave the principal evidence against him when he was found guilty at the Summer Assizes for distributing and uttering Bank of England notes. Kneeling down, Anderson made a fervent prayer on the gallows, meeting his fate with 'fortitude and resignation' before the executioner, who had come especially from the castle to carry out his job. That executioner was William Curry, himself a convicted felon who had twice escaped sentence of death.

CHAPTER SIX

IT'S ALL RELATIVE: KEEPING IT IN THE FAMILY

'God gave us our relatives; thank God we can choose our friends.'

- Ethel Watts Mumford

Since the dawn of civilisation and the advent of co-habiting familial groups, the domestic stresses of near relations and family life has always existed. One family member committing a crime against another is not a new notion, and violence and murder committed within the family circle carried the same serious social taboo in the past as it does to the present day.

Victorian family in a slum area of York. (Courtesy of York Museums Trust, York Art Gallery)

While the instances of familial murder may have fluctuated, subject to the varying social and economic pressures governing the size and circumstance of households past, the following cases amply attest to the fact that the good folk of York were in no way immune to the murderous inclinations engendered by the sentiment expressed in the old adage, 'You can choose your friends, but you can't choose your family.'

Life Partners

Intimate associations dictate that husbands and wives, lovers and sweethearts always have been and always will be prone to the odd spot of discord, it's only human. Unfortunately, in some instances these moments of conflict become escalated and can end in tears – maybe even blood.

We start with an ending so to speak, as the boyfriend and murderer of Juliet Wood was in fact the last person to be executed at York Prison in 1896 – a dubious claim to fame if ever there was one. August Carlsen, a forty-three-year-old Swedish seaman, was justly found guilty of Juliet's murder committed in the summer of that year. Though natives of Hull and living in Myton Street near the docks, at that time Hull fell within the East Riding of Yorkshire and therefore Carlsen was tried at York. Juliet worked as a part-time prostitute, which inflamed Carlsen's jealousy whenever he was ashore, and he was known to be repeatedly violent towards her. Incredibly, the sympathies of the judge and jury sitting on the case were swayed by the fact that Carlsen had been intoxicated at the time of the killing, although it was noted that the couple were said to be in an almost permanent state of inebriation. However, on the evening of 23 July matters clearly got out of control when Carlsen, presumably more intoxicated than usual, knocked on his landlord's door to tell him, 'I've just killed Juliet.' The unfortunate Juliet, aged thirty-eight, was found on the bed with her throat cut and indeed very much dead.

Recommendations for mercy were ultimately rejected by the Home Office, and no reprieve on extenuating circumstances was forthcoming, despite the request of the presiding judge and jury. Consequently, August Carlsen spent his last days in the condemned cell at York Prison on an iron bed with only the comfort of a thin straw mattress (the fireplace and

Interior of the condemned cell at York Gaol.

rudimentary toilet were later additions to the Victorian cell). Carlsen was hanged on Tuesday, 22 December 1896.

Nearly forty years previous to Carlsen's untimely end, another throat-cutting boyfriend to grace the scaffold outside York Prison was one John Taylor Whitworth. His demise proved a big draw in terms of audience numbers, with an estimated 5,000 spectators turning out to watch him hang on the afternoon of 8 January 1859.

Whitworth was convicted of murdering his sweetheart Sally Hare, a servant girl whose throat he had cut on 1 October 1858, after an altercation arising from his suspicions that Sally was paying marked attentions to another man, and exacerbated by her refusal of Whitworth's sexual demands.

The verdict of 'wilful murder' returned against Whitworth, a twenty-two-year-old assistant shepherd and farm servant, must have rested primarily on the evidence Sally gave in the statement she made shortly before dying of the wounds inflicted on her by her controlling and possessive partner:

The prisoner and I have kept company for about three years. Last night, the 30th of September, he came to see me. My mistress went to bed and left us up together in the kitchen. My master went to bed about eight o'clock. The prisoner and I sat quietly together till about one o'clock, and no angry words passed between us. About one o'clock he left the house to start for home, and asked me to accompany him a short distance. It was a beautiful starlit night, and I consented. We left the house together and got as far as the little common. He then accused me of going with another young man, whose name he did not mention. We had some words about it, and he asked me to take poison. He said, 'If you will take some, I will take some too, and we can die together'. I said I would not. He said, 'If you don't, I will kill you'. I said, 'Though you do kill me, I won't take any'. Immediately on leaving the house, and before he accused me of infidelity, he had attempted to take improper liberties with me, and had made indecent proposals to me. I would not accede to his proposals, and he then accused me of going with another man. After I refused to take the poison he got hold of me, threw me on the ground, put his knee upon me, pulled out a knife, opened it, and cut my throat. Before he cut me I implored him not to kill me, but he put one hand on my mouth, and with the other cut my throat. I got the knife out of his hand and managed to get up, but in the struggle I cut my hands and fingers very much. When I had got up he stabbed me in the throat with the knife, and I got hold of his hair, threw him backwards, and so managed to escape. When I was on the ground, and endeavouring to rise, he stamped upon my head with his foot two or three times. I ran home, bleeding all the way, and went straight to my mistress's bedroom. I said that Whitworth had tried to murder me. My mistress got up and endeavoured to stop the bleeding with some clothes, and I was put to bed, where I have been ever since.

One wonders, if Sally had been in agreement with Whitworth's suggested suicide pact whether he would actually have gone through with it. However, his behaviour after Sally's refusal was clearly very far removed from that of any romantic Romeo's to an un-obliging Juliet, as his ensuing violence and subsequent fatal assault on Sally proved.

Whitworth's behaviour after the crime did seem to be remorseful. While in police custody he asked to see Sally's body and on being admitted to the room where she laid, kissed her three times in a very affected manner. However, no amount of contrite, conscience-stricken behaviour could atone for his taking

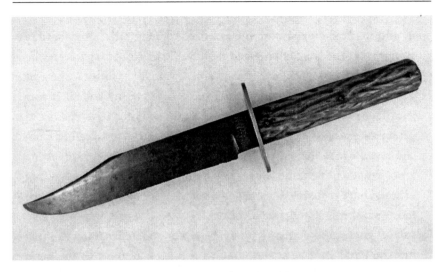

Such a sharp blade cut short Sally's existence at the hands of her 'lover'.

Sally's life, and Whitworth's feeble defence of himself did nothing to help his case, as his following statement demonstrates:

The girl went out with me from the house, and we went together as far as we had often gone before, and then we stopped for a short time. She asked me when I was going with her to the feast at Tattershall Thorpe, and I said I thought there was no good me going there, and that she did not want me. She said if I did not care for her, she did not care for me. I said we have not been long together, but I hope to be comfortable. We got to further words, and I told her I thought she went with another man. She said before she would tell me she would lose her life. I said I did not wish to go with anyone else while she went with me. I then asked her if she would go any further, and she said she would not. She said, 'We will part as we have always done before.' She then told me to sit down and she would sit on my knee. I sat down, with my feet in the hollow of the ground, and she sat on my knee. When she sat down she said, 'What have you got here?' I said 'It's my knife.' She asked me to let her look at it, and I asked her what for. She said she thought it was as much her knife as mine, and then she got the knife out of my hand and opened it. I said she should not open it, and that I should shut it again. I tried to get it out of her hand to shut it, and she said before I should have it she would try for her life. I tried to get the knife again, and it came through her fingers. She said, 'Bill, you have cut my fingers' and I said, 'I'll have my knife if it cuts your face off.' She then said, 'Then, you shall try for it.' So I tried to get it again, and she got hold of the hair of my head. I asked her what she meant, and she said if I would not let her go she would let me know what she meant. I said we had better part good friends, and that I should have my knife. She then got hold of my hair again, and pulled me down. I rolled her twice over and her head caught my feet. I said I should not stand that, and she said she would not give into me. I told her she had better be starting, and she struck at me with the knife in her hand. I tried to keep her off my face, and it went on my jacket sleeve. I tried to get the knife again, but she had fast hold of it, and she said she would not part with it. Rolling about together, the knife went in the side of her face, and I tried to get it out of her hand. She stuck to it fast, and threw me over again. She then said, 'Oh, Bill, the knife has run into my neck.' I said, 'I cannot help it; you should have let go of the knife, and let me go.' She said, 'Let's get up, and I will give you a kiss and let you go.' So we got up, and I said, 'Come, then, my lass, put your arms round my neck and I'll give you a kiss.' Then she came to me and said, 'Oh, Bill,' I said, 'What, my lass?' She said, 'My throat's cut.' I asked her what with, and she said, 'This knife here.' She said, 'I will give you a kiss for the last.' I said, 'Come, then,' and while I put my arms round her neck she struck the knife right at my throat, and said, 'Go to hell with you, Bill.' I then fell on my back, and she ran away. When I got up I saw no one, and made the best of my way home. I was taken to the lockup, and did not know what it was for till this morning, when they told me it was for cutting the throat of Sally Hare. I was taken to see her, and gave her three kisses, and was then brought away.

The jury returned a verdict of 'wilful murder' against Whitworth, who was accordingly committed by the coroner to take his trial at the ensuing York Assizes. Despite Whitworth's initial protestations that Sally's death was an accident, he admitted his guilt while being held at York Castle. After he was hanged, Whitworth was interred within the castle precincts.

The Burning Issue of Inequality in Execution

While hanging was the standard capital punishment for a husband who murdered his wife, wives found guilty of murdering their husbands were executed by strangulation and burning at the stake. A woman who killed her husband was thought to have broken the 'natural hierarchy' – it was the accepted norm that men ranked above women in the scheme of things, and as such, a wife was not only guilty of murder but also of petty treason, which carried the more severe penalty at the stake.

Burnings did not feature as a frequent execution spectacle at York, and while usually associated as a punishment for witchcraft, there were only four instances of women being burnt for petty treason. Elizabeth Boardingham was the last woman to be burned at the stake in York, at Tyburn on 20 March 1776. The judge presiding over Elizabeth's case, Sir Henry Gould, particularly alluded to the matter of 'natural hierarchy' when he summed up his sentencing thus:

The law of man, consistent with that of the gospel, has determined, that there is a submission due from the wife to her husband, and a degree of subordination the husband has over the wife, therefore constitutes a degree of allegiance from the wife to her husband, as her head, which, if she transgresses, is called by the

Thankfully, only effigies are burnt today – a grim reminder of past horrific execution methods.

law, a small, or light degree of treason. For this offence, and in order to deter women from breaking their marriage vows (and from the evidence we have heard given, you have done), the law has stamped a punishment full of ignominy upon such offenders.

Sir Henry further remarked that:

The sentence which the law obliges me to pass upon you, is that you, Elizabeth Boardingham, shall be led from this to the gaol from whence you came, and from thence upon Wednesday next, you shall be drawn upon a hurdle to the place of execution, and there you are to be burnt with fire till you are dead, and your body consumed to ashes. There is nevertheless, such a spirit of lenity in the common law of this country, tho' this is the sentence you have received, and, for my own part do not believe that sentence could ever be more properly executed in the strict letter thereof, than upon you, however severe the punishment is, that you, who have been found guilty of a crime of the greatest magnitude, are condemned to undergo, the law has allowed some mitigation – you are first to be strangled at a stake, and then to be burnt with fire. You have reason to admire the excellency of that constitution by which you have been tried and found guilty.

Quite how Elizabeth was expected to appreciate the 'spirit of lenity in the common law' that Sir Henry thought she should is beyond modern comprehension, but the contemporary view of Elizabeth's crime was coloured entirely by the patriarchal society of the eighteenth century, appallingly unfair though that reality may have been.

Elizabeth Boardingham was not condemned alone, however, as Thomas Aikney, her lover and accomplice in murdering her husband John, was sentenced to death also – but by hanging of course.

Elizabeth's late husband John Boardingham was no stranger to York Gaol himself, having spent frequent spells in prison for smuggling, leaving Elizabeth alone to raise their five children. In October 1775, still in her early thirties and understandably dissatisfied with her feckless and unreliable husband, Elizabeth ran away to Lincolnshire with Aikney, leaving the care of her children to her husband. However, whether through guilt or worry at leaving her offspring in such questionable custody, within three months Elizabeth had returned to the marital home. The reconciliation was flimsy to say the least, and with Elizabeth's patience worn through she pressured Aikney into agreeing to murder her husband. On the night of 13 February 1776, Aikney went to the Boardingham residence and stabbed John twice before running away. John managed to stagger out in to the street and, pulling the knife from his body, shouted, 'Murder! Murder!' before collapsing dead.

Elizabeth and her lover were soon arrested, and Aikney admitted to murdering John Boardingham but accused Elizabeth of repeatedly coercing him to do so. They were both found guilty and scheduled for execution on the same day. Elizabeth was variously described as 'showy' and 'worthless', and was somewhat younger in years than her husband, she was also portrayed in the press at the time as a broad, tough woman. When it came to the time of their execution, observers claimed that Elizabeth shook Aikney's hand as they parted for the last time, although Rede's *York Castle In The Nineteenth Century* has an account which states that, 'An inhabitant of York, who perfectly remembers the occurrence, informs us "That her associate in crime, a very young man, was hanged as an accessory", and that Elizabeth turned to him and asked him to kiss her at the stake, which he refused.'

The three other cases of women being burnt in York for the petty treason of murdering their husbands before the execution of Elizabeth Boardingham, were those of Elizabeth Webster in 1744, Mary Ellah in 1757 and Ann Sowerby in 1767.

Webster was tried for the poisoning of her husband John and convicted at the Summer Assizes of 1743. However, because Elizabeth was pregnant her execution was held over until after the birth of her son, who was christened William in York Castle Gaol on Michaelmas Day, 29 September 1743. Elizabeth's sentence was finally carried out on 5 March 1744. There is no record as to what became of the orphaned William Webster. While a prison birth in the eighteenth century was not the most auspicious of beginnings for a child, some were lucky enough to receive support for their upkeep from the Three Ridings of York until old enough to be put out to an apprenticeship, usually around twelve years of age.

Mary Ellah, a native of Broomfleet in the East Riding, was found guilty of murdering her husband with an axe, apparently prompted by a 'fit of jealous excitement'. She was strangled and burned at the stake on Monday, 28 March 1757. Details of Mary's crime were apparently deemed news-worthy outside of the county, and reported as far afield as Worcester in the *Berrow's Worcester Journal*, where the County News section mentioned that, 'On Friday last, Mary Ellah, of Broomfleet in the East Riding, was committed to the said Gaol, upon the Coroner's Warrant, for the Murder

'strangled and burned at the stake'

of Thomas Ellah, her Husband, by giving him a Blow on his Temples with an Axe.' While the *London Chronicle* recorded that 'Yesterday, Mary Ellah who was convicted of the Murder of her Husband Thomas Ellah, was burnt, Pursuant to her sentence. She confessed the Crime for which she suffered, and died penitent.'

Ann Sowerby poisoned her husband Timothy in collusion with one John Douglas. Although Douglas was acquitted, Ann was executed by strangulation and burning at the stake. Prior to being removed from her cell for execution, Ann protested that Douglas had supplied her with the poison nux vomica, and that she had burned the remainder of the substance. She further claimed that Douglas had supplied her with more poison, this time arsenic, some days later and assisted her with mixing it in with some curds that she fed to her husband for breakfast, resulting in his death a few hours later. Possibly Ann (and for that matter Douglas) may have thought the latter poison was a more viable option – arsenic's popularity as a poison (before the advent of forensic testing) lay in its virtual tastelessness, a supposedly faintly sweet and metallic taste easily masked by food, as opposed to the strong, bitter taste of nux vomica. Drawn on a hurdle through the streets to the Tyburn, Ann at the last acknowledged the justness of her sentence and 'died penitent'.

Parents and Siblings

A brutal case of patricide occurred around noon on 18 July 1803. When Mr Oldroyd senior complained of feeling unwell and went to lay down in his parlour, his son Benjamin (aged forty-six) subsequently seized his father and fastened a rope around his neck, suspending the helpless old man from a nail some 7ft from the ground.

It was heavily inferred that Mrs Oldroyd was an accessory to the murder of her husband, as neither mother nor son saw fit to raise the alarm until six o'clock that evening. It was assumed that the delay between the murder and the report of Joseph Oldroyd's 'suicide' was occasioned by Benjamin and his mother dragging the body into the garden and fastening the corpse to a cherry tree in an attempt to make it appear that Mr Oldroyd had taken his own life, (although it was observed that the tree was not substantial enough to have borne the body). Mrs Oldroyd maintained that her husband had made many attempts on his own life before and had been in 'a desponding way for two years', and that she believed he had hanged himself as he had often told her he would.

While Benjamin was described as being of 'very weak intellect', the court decided he was capable of distinguishing right from wrong, and he was eventually found guilty of the murder of his father at the Spring Assizes of 1804. Until the sentence was confirmed, Benjamin had been of a placid demeanour while held in York Prison. However, on 20 May when the order of execution was confirmed, Oldroyd's demeanour changed, and when it came to the day of execution on 27 May Benjamin refused to join in the prayers. On the platform his conduct was described as 'dreadful', and he physically resisted being hanged, 'He fought and struggled with the officers of justice until from exhaustion, he fell upon his face; yelling and struggling, he was encircled in the fatal noose, and the drop fell.'

An Insistent Sister: The 'Kirklington Murderer'

On 18 August 1874 at 2.30 a.m., twenty-nine-year-old William Jackson, formerly a private in the 77th Regiment of Foot, confessed in the condemned cell of York Gaol that he was responsible for the murder of his sixteen-year-old-sister Elizabeth. On 5 May that year, Jackson's sister had been accompanying her brother on the initial leg of his outward journey from the family home in Kirklington, as he went to seek work. She was desperate for him to take her along with him but Jackson had refused, and, in spite of his sister's pleas, tried to make her see the sense in her waiting for him to send for her once he had secured a position. Elizabeth, who was terribly upset, continued to follow her brother, who on his own admission, 'Opened my black bag and took out my razor, and cut my sister Lizzie's throat. She screamed out when the blood flew out.' Lizzie dropped to the footpath, and on realisation of what he had done Jackson fled the scene, but was arrested in Bishop Aukland the following Saturday.

A cut-throat razor from the 1870s – a convenient instrument to silence Jackson's sister.

Utterly remorseful for his actions, Jackson, who became known as the 'Kirklington Murderer', paid the ultimate penalty later that day after his confession. His was the first execution to take place within the castle grounds, after Parliament passed the Capital Punishment (Amendment) Act ending public hangings in 1868. A black flag was hoisted over Clifford's Tower indicating that Jackson had been hanged and was lowered once again when his body had been cut down.

INFANTICIDE AND 'PLEADING THE BELLY'

In the Family Way

'Yea, mothers have with desperate hands wrought harm. To little lives which their own bosoms lent.'

Maturin

In the past, stillbirths and what we now class as cot deaths must have been far more prevalent, particularly with the lack of medical knowledge to remedy prenatal problems and when a parents' own bed might have been the only place where a poor mother and father could offer warmth to their baby. Natural deaths and 'over-layings' – where an infant would be accidentally suffocated in the parental bed – must then have been difficult to distinguish from deliberate infanticide by suffocation, or the result of fatal negligence. Backstreet abortions resulting in a deliberately induced miscarriage would also be passed off as stillbirths.

Consequently, proving infanticide was something of a problem, and while failure to disclose a stillbirth was made a capital offence in 1624, it was not until 1803 that the law on infanticide was revised, with proof of murder now a requirement to secure a conviction. In circumstances where a murder charge was unlikely to stick, the accused could alternatively be charged with concealment of birth instead, punishable by a maximum of two years' imprisonment. (In cases where the defendant was charged with infanticide the jury was empowered to return 'concealment of birth' as a lesser verdict.)

Of course, procuring or performing unlawful abortions also fell within this criminal sphere. Prior to 1803, having an abortion or the offence of 'attempting to induce a miscarriage' was punishable by a fine or a short term of imprisonment – in fact, abortions carried out before the 'quickening' (where the mother could feel the movement of the foetus around the thirteen-week mark) would go entirely unpunished. While abortion laws were progressively tightened as the nineteenth century progressed, with the proviso concerning 'quickening' removed in 1837, it was not until after the passing of the 1861 Offence Against the Person Act that the pregnant woman herself (as opposed to the abortionist) could be prosecuted under the law. The effects of poverty, ineffective contraception, the incidence of birth defects and attitudes to illegitimacy as well as prostitution all ensured a steady stream of offenders coming before the assizes.

On Monday, 1 August 1803, nineteen-year-old Martha Chapel was executed upon the New Drop behind the castle walls for the wilful murder of her illegitimate child, born some six weeks prior. Martha, described as a 'fine-looking young woman and industrious and good-tempered', was a domestic servant. Though the identity of the child's father was never disclosed, some harboured a suspicion that Martha's employer was responsible. Three or

Drawing from a thirteenth-century manuscript of Pseudo-Apuleius's *Herbarium*, depicting the preparations for an abortion by the administration of a concoction made from Pennyroyal, historically a popular herbal abortifacient.

A domestic scene recreated by York Castle Museum – in such circumstances poor families lived and died.

four months before her baby's due date, Martha took up a new position – possibly forced to move on by her former and culpable employer, or fleeing before her condition became obviously visible. Whatever her reasons, she told nobody she was expecting (and of course there is always the possibility she was not even aware of the pregnancy herself). On 15th June, Martha absented herself, claiming she felt unwell. Unattended, she subsequently gave birth to a baby girl, who was found dead shortly afterwards.

While maintaining her innocence, insisting that any harm done to the child was the consequence of pain delirium and the panic of manually trying to hasten her own self-delivery, the testimony of a doctor damned Martha, claiming that she must have killed the baby with her own hands.

Quoted at her trial as saying, 'I am a wretched woman, it was my child. I never meant it harm ... I loved my child before I saw it.' It took the jury only ten minutes of deliberation to find Martha guilty. After the execution, Martha's body was given over for dissection.

Progress in attitudes toward illegitimacy and the recognition that childbirth could have a detrimental psychological effect on the mother were a long-time forming, and it wasn't until 1922 that the law was changed, preventing any new mother receiving the death penalty for infanticide. Tragically, this was too far in the future to have any bearing on the case of Mary Thorpe, who was hanged on Monday, 17 March 1800 at the York Tyburn for drowning her week-old illegitimate son. While the court accepted that Mary was suffering from 'milk fever' (a common eighteenth-century term for mastitis), such conditions, as well as postnatal depression, were not recognised as extenuating circumstances and the jurors did not deem that Mary's condition had any bearing on her mental well-being or

'drowning her week-old illegitimate son'

that it significantly affected her subsequent actions. Mary was described as a 'decent, respectable-looking young woman,' who, 'during the whole of her confinement in the castle, manifested the most sincere contrition for the dreadful crime of which she had been found guilty.' Mary, who was not more than twenty-one years of age, was executed, alongside one Michael Simpson who had been found guilty of poisoning. Incidentally, Simpson asserted his innocence to the last, and eighteen months later the confession of the real murderer proved that Michael Simpson had been telling the truth all along. Did two innocent people hang that day?

The case of another unwanted infant being drowned culminated in the execution of Lydia Dickenson, who, on 26 February 1784, had murdered 'her female bastard child by drowning it in a pond'. Her execution on Monday, 22 March was one of those which proved a great draw, as the nineteen-year-old Lydia was hanged at the Tyburn 'in the presence of a large concourse of people'.

Twenty-three-year-old Ann Haywood's murder of her illegitimate child warranted a chapter in Leman Thomas Rede's *York Castle*, published in 1831. The account of Ann's life and trial numbering among the high profile capital offenders that Rede included in his 'account of all the principal offences committed in Yorkshire from the year 1800 to the present period.' Described as the daughter of labouring people, Ann was apparently 'brought up with very little attention devoted to her morals' (perhaps a judgment made with hindsight). She went into service when she was aged thirteen, but her 'violent temper' was the cause of her losing more than one position. It was during one of these periods of unemployment in 1802 that Ann met the father of her future child. Sadly, while Ann was hopeful that the relationship would develop into a matrimonial commitment the young man had other ideas, and 'taking advantage of the feeling that his attention had inspired' nature took its course, and in 1804 Ann found herself pregnant and alone. Ann was forced to leave her position in July as there was already some suspicion about her condition, but found another place in service, with the Roodhouse family of Rotherham. She was so adept at dressing to conceal her increasing bulk that not even her fellow servants suspected her pregnancy.

That was until the morning of 30 November, when Ann's labour began and she subsequently gave birth unaided in an outhouse, where she later stabbed her newborn daughter to death. She then concealed the body and fabricated the plausible excuse of preparing a fowl for the pot to account for the presence of bloodstains on her person and on the outhouse floor. However, Mrs Roodhouse's intuition led her to believe otherwise and a subsequent search revealed the infant's buried body.

At the inquest Ann confessed the child was hers, but denied murder. Held in York Castle until the next Spring Assizes, at her trial Ann pleaded 'not guilty'. But the evidence was stacked against her, and the 'body of a very large, full-grown newborn, female infant' found 'in a very lacerated state' coupled with the blood-smeared pen knife found concealed under Ann's bed was enough to condemn her. After the judge's summing up, the verdict of 'guilty' was immediately returned by the jury, probably helped along by the examining surgeon's description of the wounds that had been inflicted on the baby, namely, 'Two small punctures on the left side of its face, a small cut on the left angle of the mouth, a puncture on the back of the right soulder [sic], and a deep incision from the right ear to within an inch and a half of the navel, by which laceration the child was disembowelled, and the collar bone and ribs entirely cut through.'

Perhaps because of the brutal way in which Ann had murdered her child (although the apparent frenzied level of the attack could have been attributed to the pain and panic induced by the self-delivery) the crowd that gathered to witness Ann's execution on Monday, 18 March 1805 at the New Drop, was described as 'unusually great' and that 'the number of females in the crowd was very great'.

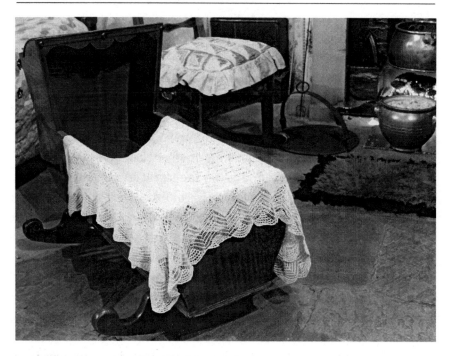

A typical infant's cot from the 1800s.

However, the termination of illegitimate offspring was not exclusively a maternal remit, as many fathers were also responsible for the act of infanticide, as was the case with John Rodda who, on 19 April 1846, murdered his eighteen-month-old daughter, Mary, by poisoning her with oil of vitriol (sulphuric acid). In this instance the motive was financial, as Rodda, a dealer and hawker of mats in Skipton, murdered his little girl for the £2 and 10s burial fee he would be entitled to receive as a member of a burial club (or 'dead clubs' as they were sometimes known). Such clubs were a popular notion in a time of high mortality rates, especially among children, and when poor working-class families were fearful that they would be unable to pay for a decent funeral for their loved ones, leaving them to rely on the local Poor Union to provide a pauper's burial, which meant interment in a common grave without a headstone.

The initial inquest into Mary's death was reported in the May, in an edition of the *Illustrated London News*, under the headline: 'A child murdered for her burial fee.' The report stated:

It appears that [John Rodda] is a member of a burial club and that he would have been entitled to 2.10s on the death of the child. Under pretence of killing vermin he purchased some oil of vitriol which he poured down the throat of his child whilst she was at home in the cradle, which caused her death. The jury returned a verdict of wilful murder against the father who was committed to York Castle, to take his trial for the horrid offence at the next assizes.

Rodda, who protested his innocence, was tried at York Castle on Friday, 17 June. The prosecutor, Mr Hall, told the jury that the accusation of murder was, 'A charge so unusual and so repugnant to the ordinary feelings of human nature that he must caution them against being prejudiced against the prisoner' – the jury returned a verdict of 'guilty' after deliberating for an hour and a half. A few days prior to his execution, Rodda, who was a Roman Catholic, made a full confession of his guilt and stated, 'that avarice was his only motive.'

The *Criminal Chronology of York Castle*, published in 1857, detailed Rodda's execution thus:

At an early hour on Saturday morning, August 8th, the workmen commenced erecting the drop in front of St George's Field, and the solemn preparations for the awful ceremony were speedily completed. At the usual hour the wretched man, with blanched cheek and dejected look – his arms pinioned – appeared on the scaffold. After spending a few minutes in prayer, the executioner proceeded to perform the duties of his office, by drawing the cap over his eyes and adjusting the rope, when the fatal bolt was withdrawn – the drop fell – a convulsive struggle ensued – and the mortal ceased to exist.

It was also reported that:

There was a large concourse of spectators in St George's Field to witness the spectacle, amongst whom were a number of the lower orders of the Irish, who had congregated to witness the last moments of their countryman.

Another father to kill his illegitimate daughter was Martin Slack, who did so by poisoning her with aqua fortis (nitric acid) claiming that the baby's mother, Elizabeth Haigh, had poisoned the child herself and framed Slack in vengeance for his refusal to marry her. Slack maintained his innocence up to the last moment, protesting, 'Mine was not the hand that administered the poison; it was given by the mother of the child.' Slack was hanged at noon on Monday, 30 March 1829 at the New Drop before a large number of spectators, with women making up a large percentage of the onlookers.

George Howe, a railway labourer from Yarm, was found guilty of the murder of his infant daughter Eliza Amelia Howe by poisoning her with oxalic acid on 25 January 1849. Eliza Amelia was Howe's daughter by his second wife who had died shortly after the child's birth the previous October. Howe's neighbours already suspected his neglectful tendencies toward the baby and so it came as no surprise when Howe was found guilty of poisoning his infant daughter with a substance that was commonly used as a cleaning agent at the time.

On Saturday, 31 March 1849 at twelve o'clock, Howe walked out on to the scaffold erected early that morning in the usual place in front of St George's Field. It was reported that:

He appeared to pray most fervently for a few minutes, after which the executioner placed the cap over his head, and put the rope in its proper position. He then withdrew the fatal bolt – the drop fell – a momentary thrill of horror passed through the immense

Eliza Amelia's existence was cut short before she could enjoy such toys.

mass of people – there were a few short heavings of the shoulders – and the body of George Howe was a lifeless piece of clay – his spirit had fled into the boundless depths of an eternity whose mysteries have now been fully developed to his criminal soul, and whose blessings, we trust, he has received through the merits of a crucified Redeemer.

Both Mother and Child

In some instances, the expectant mother was killed before the baby was even born, and in many cases it was the result of the father wishing to avoid responsibility and the financial burden for the unwanted, usually illegitimate, child.

On 21 March 1774, John Scott of Northowram poisoned his partner Hannah Stocks, mother of Scott's child and six months pregnant with their next baby. This was a particularly brutal case; Scott had forced Hannah to take arsenic at knifepoint after she refused, despite his insistence, to take a poisonous draught that would have induced a miscarriage. The couple were not married, although Scott had 'followed or kept company' with Hannah since the birth of their son some years before. Visiting Hannah the week before her death, apparently with the intent to pay a weekly allowance toward the upkeep of his son, it would seem that the realisation that there would soon be another hungry mouth to provide for proved too much for Scott, who was clearly willing to go to any length to avoid supporting a second child. He paid the ultimate price, however, when he was hanged at the Tyburn on Monday, 25 July 1774, and his body was given to the local hospital for dissection.

The hospital would gain another cadaver following the shocking case of thirty-three-year-old John Robinson, who had murdered his former servant girl, Susannah Wilson, who had been eight months pregnant. The Newgate Calendar, supposedly a moralising publication that gave vivid accounts of notorious criminals in the eighteenth and nineteenth centuries, did not fail to disappoint in this instance, giving a full report of Robinson's case:

About eight o'clock they sat down together: the deceased continued frequently to lament in the most affecting terms her unhappy situation, unconscious of the fate that awaited her. At this moment the prisoner stole unobserved behind her and, with an axe he had previously furnished himself with, gave her a mortal blow on the back of the head, which penetrated through the skull to the brain, and instantly killed her; but the prisoner, to make more sure of her death, mangled her dead body with the murderous axe, inflicting now on her lifeless corpse many deep wounds. The body was then deposited by him in the place where it was afterwards found, covered with whins.

Robinson was executed at the New Drop on Saturday, 8 August 1807 in a state of 'evinced contrition' for his crime.

John Bolton, a Lieutenant in the 1st Regiment of the West Riding Militia, though found guilty of the murder of his pregnant serving-girl Elizabeth Rainbow, cheated the crowds of the public spectacle of his hanging by taking his own life before his sentence could be carried out. Bolton had hired Elizabeth from the Foundling Hospital at Ackworth, and clearly getting her pregnant was not part of the employment plan. On the afternoon of Sunday, 21 August 1774, while his wife was out of the house visiting friends, Bolton killed Elizabeth and buried her body in his cellar. Bolton strangled the unfortunate Elizabeth with a length of cord, and her untimely death would go on to inspire a popular thirteen-verse ballad, sung to the tune of 'Fair Lady lay your costly robes aside'.

Following Bolton's trial held at the Lent Assizes at York Castle on Monday, 27 March 1775, it is recorded that the following Wednesday, on the morning designated for his hanging, Bolton had 'found means to be his own executioner in the cell' employing a garter, a piece of cord and a handkerchief to end his life – he was found between six and seven o'clock in the morning, strangled, rather than hanged, as his feet were still on the floor of the cell. The account ends with the coroner's inquest turning in a verdict of *Felo de se*, Latin for 'felon of himself', which is an archaic legal term meaning suicide, and that Bolton's body was given over to the county hospital for dissection. However, Knipe's *Criminal Chronology* states that Bolton, 'Was buried at the three lane ends near the York Barracks, at ten o'clock at night, and a stake driven through his body in the presence of the turnkeys of the castle.' This crossroads burial was in accordance with the custom and law that suicides and convicted criminals be denied burial in consecrated ground – clearly Bolton qualified on both counts.

In the nineteenth century, Rachel Crossley was murdered by William Shaw, the father of Crossley's three-year-old child while she was carrying another child by him. Considerably behind with maintenance payments (4s a week) and under increasing pressure to marry Crossley, Shaw's crime inspired the lengthy verse 'The Yorkshire Tragedy', a cautionary tale imploring 'young lovers all pray now attend' and detailing how Shaw battered the pregnant Rachel and disposed of her body down a pit:

Her body fair he mangled sore,
But still she was alive,
And down a pit full sixty yards,
To hide her did contrive.
When the colliers went to work,
They stagger'd to behold
A female form upon the ground,
All bloody, wet and cold.

Shaw had murdered twenty-two-year-old Rachel on 9 March 1830, and in this instance the law and retribution were swift. The accused was tried on the morning of 2 April in an 'intensely crowded' courtroom and despite his plea of not guilty Shaw was hanged at the New Drop the following Monday.

Yet more fathers were driven to the most deplorable of actions in the face of maintenance demands and arrears of upkeep payments. On 5 February 1814, Robert Turner poisoned Margaret Appleby, who was pregnant with his child, because she was on the point of registering a claim for child maintenance. It was suggested after the trial that Turner had in fact intended merely to induce an abortion with the potion he gave to Margaret. She had readily imbibed it when Turner offered her a rum and warm water procured from a nearby alehouse after Turner had waylaid Margaret on her way to the magistrates, where she intended to secure the order to commence upkeep. Immediately after taking the drink, Margaret 'was seized with violent vomiting' and with the limited effectiveness of medical intervention at that time, Margaret vomited continually until she died seven days later, on 12 February.

Turner had already absconded on the day he had administered the poison to Margaret, but was apparently 'afterwards found concealed in a cupboard in South Shields'. Denying his guilt, stating that he had administered no poison and the child was not even his, Turner was executed at the New Drop on the 31 March 1814, protesting his innocence to the last. Of course, it may well have been that Turner himself was unaware of the true nature of the substance he had given to the unfortunate Margaret Appleby, who nevertheless died in agony.

'Pleading the Belly'

'Why, she may plead her Belly at worst; to my Knowledge she hath taken care of that Security. But, as the Wench is very active and industrious, you may satisfy her that I'll soften the Evidence.'

- *The Beggar's Opera* (1765) Act I, Scene 21

Under English common law 'pleading the belly' permitted women in the later stages of pregnancy to be reprieved of their death sentences until after the delivery of the child. The plea did not constitute a defence and could only be made after a guilty verdict had been passed, and verification was determined by a 'jury of matrons'. If found to be 'quick with child' (that is, the movements of the foetus could be detected), a reprieve would be granted. Records indicate that this plea was exercised as early as 1228, but was eventually rendered obsolete with the passing of the Sentence of Death (Expectant Mothers) Act in 1931.

Women granted such a reprieve were often subsequently granted pardons or had their sentences commuted to transportation, which naturally left the system open to abuse. The practice of selecting a jury of matrons from the courtroom observers opened up the opportunity for planting sympathetic accomplices in the public gallery, causing one eighteenth-century commentator to complain that female felons would have, 'Matrons of [their] own Profession ready at hand, who, right or wrong, bring their wicked Companions quick with Child to the great Impediment of Justice.'

In Daniel Defoe's *Moll Flanders*, written in 1721, one character successfully pleads her belly despite being 'no more with child than the judge that tried [her].' And John Gay's *The Beggar's Opera*, has the character 'Flich' making an extra income as a 'child getter ... helping the ladies to a pregnancy against their being called down to sentence.'

In an attempt to limit the abuse of the system, the law decreed that no woman could be granted a second reprieve on an original sentence passed if she were later found to be with child, even if they were actually pregnant. In addition, the gaoler or local sheriff in charge of any female prisoner falling pregnant while held in their custody was subject to a fine.

Elizabeth Cahill had indulged in a spot of pickpocketing in Leeds Market on New Year's Eve 1728. After languishing in gaol for some time, she was reprieved on successfully pleading her belly and her daughter Ann was baptised in York Castle on 15 May 1733. However, Elizabeth's sentence of transportation was reinstated in the summer of 1735.

Naomi Hollings had been sentenced to death at the Lent Assizes of 1739 for the theft of money and goods after breaking and entering into a private dwelling house. Again, she was reprieved of her execution on successfully pleading her belly, and, on 13 June 1739, Naomi's son was christened Castellus in York Castle, an apt name given the child's place of birth. Her sentence was, however, reinstated and she was transported the following summer of 1740.

Not all children were left motherless though, as the case of Mary Burgan attests. She was originally convicted in 1705 of killing her first baby, for which she would ordinarily have hanged, and while awaiting trial she became pregnant again, in all probability by the turnkey, Thomas Ward. Mary was allowed to live in the prison with her son Thomas, who grew up in York Castle Gaol supported by payments made by the Three Ridings until 1718, when he was put out to apprenticeship at the age of twelve. Mary had been listed as a 'reprieve' in the Calendar of Felons for York Castle 1707, and her sentence was subsequently changed to that of transportation. It appears, however, she was then released locally under Queen Anne's general pardon of 1710.

CHAPTER EIGHT

REBELS, RIOTERS & REFORMERS

Viewed as subversive, rabble-rousing, insurgent and insurrectionist, whether the following individuals were all or any of these things they certainly left their mark on York's history, and they certainly felt the full weight of the law, either at the edge of the executioner's blade or dangling from a rope.

Rebellious Archbishop of York

A noteworthy act of rebellion on the part of a Yorkshireman against the reigning monarch was that of Richard Scrope, fourth son of Henry, first Baron Scrope of Masham, who rose to become Archbishop of York. Becoming deeply involved in the rebellion against King Henry IV in the early years, after his usurpation of the throne from Richard II in 1399, the Archbishop made his loyalties clear when he preached against the King in the minster. The response of 'almost all the citizens of York capable of bearing arms' saw the armour-clad archbishop heading up an 8,000-strong rebel army, who at the end of May 1405 faced a larger loyalist army on Shipton Moor. Either in the light of peaceful scruples or plain common sense in the face of a greater opposing force, Scrope disbanded his force in exchange for a truce, only to be immediately arrested afterward.

Detail from the east window of All Saints' Church in Bolton Percy, depicting a canonised Archbishop above the coat of arms of Archbishop Richard Scrope of York.

King Henry IV himself travelled to Bishopthorpe Palace, the seat of the Archbishops of York, for the trial in the Great Hall where Scrope was found guilty of treason. He was executed with a sword in a barley field near St Clements Nunnery, Clementhorpe, which is overlooked today by Bitch Daughter Tower on the section of the city wall between Baile Hill and Victoria Bar. Scrope begged the headsman to strike five blows at his neck in recognition of the five sacred wounds of Christ, and after kissing his executioner three times, commended his spirit to God and bent his neck for the sword. As Scrope's head fell with the final severing fifth stroke, some claimed to see a smile still over his features. Scrope was buried in the Lady Chapel of the minster and afterwards was somewhat venerated as an unofficial saint, his tomb becoming something of a shrine.

Riot Over the Red Tower

Built in 1490, after a rebellion against King Henry VII, the Red Tower forms the only section of York's city wall to be constructed from brick. The use of such building materials did not sit well with the local stone

The Red Tower.

masons, however, who usually undertook the majority of the construction work on the city's walls and buildings. Subsequently, a dispute erupted between the tilers who were employed to build the tower, and the masons, who resented being done out of the job. In retaliation, the riotous masons

'murder and mutilation'

smashed the tools and kilns of the tilers and attempted to sabotage the construction of the tower. Their violent actions eventually culminated in the murder and mutilation (including his emasculation) of the master tiler, John Partick. The masons were prosecuted, including York Minster' master mason William Hindley, however, after seeking sanctuary in the minster precinct, all those accused escaped conviction.

In Search of His Head: The 7th Earl of Northumberland

The Rising of the North of 1569, also called the 'Northern Rebellion', was an unsuccessful attempt on the part of Catholic nobles from the north of England to replace the Protestant Queen Elizabeth I with her Catholic cousin Mary, Queen of Scots. Many English Catholics supported Mary's claim, especially in view of the religious persecutions they were suffering under Elizabeth's rule, and the feeling ran especially strong in the north, where several of the most powerful nobles were Catholics.

Thomas Percy, 7th Earl of Northumberland was one such powerful noble, and as a staunch Catholic led the rebellion in collusion with Charles Neville, 6th Earl of Westmorland. By November 1569, the rebels were in occupation of Durham and, flouting the laws prohibiting Catholic worship there, celebrated Mass at Durham Cathedral.

On hearing that a large force had been raised to oppose them the rebel leaders abandoned their plans to besiege York, and while they successfully captured Barnard Castle, in the face of diminishing popular support, they retreated northward and finally dispersed before fleeing to Scotland.

Percy was, however, betrayed and captured. He was dragged to York in chains and both the Pope and King Phillip of Spain failed to buy Percy's stay of execution, so he was beheaded on York's Pavement on

THE PAVEMENT

So called as early as 1378. Perhaps one of the first medieval streets in the City to have a paved way. It was the scene of public markets and gatherings, proclamations and punishments. Thomas Percy, Earl of Northumberland was beheaded here on 22nd. August 1572. At the restoration of King Charles II in 1660 the effigy of Oliver Cromwell was hung and later burnt here.

The Pavement was the venue for commercial, civic and communal activities, as well as public publishments and executions.

22 August 1572. The venue for a higher class of execution, a new scaffold was built at the Pavement especially for the occasion – 25ft long by 15ft broad and 12ft high. Mounting the scaffold with a firm step, Percy looked about him for a short time, spoke to the Sheriff and Chaplain of the Castle and addressed the spectators for about 15 minutes. After praying for a short time he silently shook hands with those on the scaffold then knelt down, facing east, and after laying his head on the block he signalled to the executioner, who struck off his head with one blow of the axe. Percy's sword had been symbolically broken at the altar of nearby St Crux Church, and his body was carried there by his servants and buried in the churchyard in an unmarked grave. However, as befitted the fate of a convicted traitor, his head was set upon a spike at Micklegate Bar, where it remained as a grim reminder for two years until it was stolen and allegedly buried by a sympathiser to Percy's cause in an unknown city churchyard. It is said that the final resting place of the Earl's head is in the churchyard of Holy Trinity, Goodramgate, and that after nightfall the ethereal spectre of Thomas Percy can still be seen vainly searching for his severed head.

The Jacobite Rebellion

York's involvement with the Jacobite rebellions between 1715 and 1745 was limited. After the first rebellion in 1715 some of the prominent rebels were held at York Castle, but overall the prevailing feeling within the city was one of anti-Jacobitism. In 1745, the Archbishop of York preached in the minster against 'Bonnie Prince Charlie's' attempt to seize the throne, and preparations were made to defend York against an attack by Stuart forces. A group of volunteers called the Yorkshire Association formed and measures were taken to strengthen the city walls, although these precautions were never actually put to the test.

After the rebels were finally defeated and crushed in 1746 by Prince William, Duke of Cumberland, also known as 'The Butcher of Culloden', the City of York sent its congratulations to his father, King George II, and the Duke of Cumberland was invited to accept the Freedom of the City, as well as being awarded with a hundred guineas in a gold box.

Of the Jacobite prisoners brought down to York Castle Gaol from Scotland for trial, seventy were sentenced to death. However, at the last moment a reprieve came through for most, but not all of them, and it was decided that lots were to be drawn. Those with the luck of the draw escaped the death penalty and were transported to the Colonies. Twenty-two men, however, were left to suffer execution, but even then in some cases a reprieve was given, and in one instance it was offered so late that John Jellons was actually being dragged toward the gallows along Castlegate when it came through. The rest were hanged, drawn and quartered, and while York's sympathies for the rebels were not apparently strong, the barbarity of their punishment so appalled many that this was the last time it was carried out in the city. In spite of public sensitivities though, two of the rebel heads were still put up for display on Micklegate Bar, and though this was also the last instance of a traitor's head being paraded over the primary entrance to the city, the severed heads of William Connolly and James Mayne's remained on spikes for eight years, until they were stolen in 1754 by two Jacobite sympathizers – William Arundel and an unnamed Irish tailor. Arundel was fined and imprisoned in the gaol on Old Ouse Bridge, and while York City Council offered a large reward for their return, the missing heads were never recovered. In a later

Micklegate Bar.

macabre twist to the Jacobites' fate, when workmen were digging a new drain at the back of York Castle Gaol they discovered the remains of about twenty bodies, some of the skeletons were minus skulls and the bones were disjointed; it is believed that the remains were those of the executed rebels.

While the city walls had been strengthened and guarded in anticipation of a Jacobite attack in 1745, they were again defended for the last time in 1757 when rioters protesting at taxation to support the militia threatened the security of the city. Enforced conscription by the Militia Ballot in the face of insufficient volunteers was almost universally detested by the civilian population and also the cause of widespread rioting. Of those imprisoned in York Castle charged with treason, some died before even reaching trial at the Lent Assizes in 1758, and some of the survivers were sentenced to transportation but one rioter, Robert Cole, was executed at York on May Day 1758 for 'levying war against the King', which is a charge connected with a riotous breach of the Militia Act.

Luddites

In the early nineteenth century, the English cloth trade was in a depressed state due to the war with France. In an economic climate where unemployment often meant destitution and starvation, the further threat of mechanisation, the undermining of wages and the use of unskilled labour – while a driving factor in the Industrial Revolution – had a hugely detrimental impact on the lives and livelihoods of skilled artisans, such as the textile workers in Nottinghamshire, Yorkshire and Lancashire. With trades and communities facing extinction, in an attempt to halt the changes in the textile industry the Luddites came into being. It is generally thought that the term 'Luddite' alluded to their apocryphal leader, known as General Ludd or King Ludd, in whose name their demands and proclamations were issued, however, the name is also said to derive from an apprentice weaver called Ned Ludd who some years earlier had been beaten by his master for smashing a loom in a rage.

The catalyst for the transition from demonstration to organised violence came in 1809 when, under pressure from manufacturers, Parliament repealed legislation that had formerly protected textile workers from 'gig mills' (machines invented in the sixteenth century that could perform some aspects of woollen finishing work). The Yorkshire Luddites were led by the highly skilled finishers of woollen cloth, known as croppers, who were able to command a much higher wage for their work.

Unable to redress their grievances by legal or democratic means, the Luddite uprising began in November 1811 in Nottingham, spreading to Yorkshire and Lancashire in early 1812. The usual tactic was to demand the removal of the mechanised frame from the workplace and if this was ignored the Luddites would use large sledgehammers to smash the machinery in nocturnal raids.

Although there were already plenty of laws on the statute books that made such an act a capital crime, in February 1812 the Government passed the Frame Breaking Act, specifically introducing the death penalty for those found to have broken frames. The Act was passed just in time to charge the sixty-four men involved in the attempted destruction of Cartwright's textile mill at Rawfold, near Brighouse, in April 1812. Held until they could come before a special judicial commission at York Castle at the beginning of January 1813, twenty-four men were convicted and seventeen sentenced to hang, while the remainder were sentenced to transportation.

The first of the Luddite executions was scheduled for Friday, 8 January. At 9 a.m., three of the convicted men, including the Yorkshire Luddite's leader George Mellor, were hanged for the murder of mill owner William Horsfall. It was reported in the press that, 'Every precaution had been taken to make a rescue impracticable. Two troops of Cavalry were drawn up at the front of the drop and the entrances to the castle were guarded by Infantry.' Executed in their irons, the ropes of the gallows were suitably adjusted to ensure the entire body of each executed man would be visible to the spectators.

Just over a week later, on 16 January, the remaining fourteen condemned Luddites were executed for their part in the raid on Cartwright's Mill – seven were hanged at 11 a.m. and the other seven at 1.30 p.m., proving a double spectacle for the mass of people assembled on St George's field to witness this multiple execution. These executions left fourteen wives widowed and fifty-seven children fatherless, eight of whom were 'turned upon the world

Frame breakers, 1812.

On display at York Castle Museum, the inscription on this sawn-off shotgun states
that it was found in a wood near Halifax, hidden with many other guns 'stolen & cut
down by Luddites'. All of the firearms were taken to York Castle when found in 1830,
and this piece is the only weapon left unclaimed by the rightful owner – incidentally
the house that Hartely was accused of raiding was only a mile from the woodland
hiding place. (Courtesy of York Museum Trust)

helpless'. Of the number of children left fatherless, seven were orphaned
when widower William Hartley was executed after being convicted on the
evidence of an informer in the company of fellow Luddites, had raided the
house of wool-stapler George Haigh for weapons held on the premises.

Hartley admitted his involvement in the raid, but denied being a ringleader or demanding and receiving any firearms. This poor tailor from
near Halifax, whose wife had died some six months previously, may have
escaped with a lesser sentence in other circumstances, but unfortunately
the authorities' vehement determination to completely crush Luddite sub-
version necessitated the brutal and final punishment of all those involved.

CHAPTER NINE

GENTLEMEN
OF THE ROAD

Before improvements in policing, road transport and banking and credit facilities led to the demise of the mounted robber from England's highways in the late 1820s, the somewhat romanticised image of the highwayman as a dashing 'gentleman thief' belied the true impact of being stopped and asked to 'stand and deliver!'

Probably the most famous (or should that be infamous?) of English highwaymen was Dick Turpin, notorious in life and in death thanks to his flamboyant final performance on the gallows at York. The legend of Dick Turpin was thoroughly romanticised by nineteenth-century novelist William Harrison Ainsworth, whose first literary success *Rookwood*, published in 1834, featured Turpin as the leading character.

A typical interpretation of a highwayman.

Turpin was born in 1705 in Hempstead, near Saffron Walden. His initial career path as a butcher led him into theft early on as the meat he sold by day had been previously stolen by night. Forced to go on the run in the depths of the Essex countryside after he was witnessed stealing two oxen, the young Turpin tried his hand at smuggling, joining a group known as the 'Essex Gang'. They were not very successful and before long pressure from customs officers curtailed this particular criminal venture, and the gang (amongst them one woman, Mary Brazier) turned to robbing remote and isolated farmhouses instead; it was only towards the end of his criminal career that Turpin became involved in actual highway robbery. By 1735, the press was regularly reporting on the exploits of the Essex Gang who were robbing their way around the Home Counties. King George II offered a £50 reward for their capture and eventually two members of the Essex Gang were apprehended by local constables – Turpin himself only narrowly escaped arrest by jumping out of an upstairs window.

After his narrow escape and a spell of living rough, Turpin struck up a working partnership with one of the most notorious highwaymen of the day, 'Captain' Tom King. His association with King proved fruitful and by 1737, the bounty on Turpin's head had been increased to £100.

However, their affiliation was abruptly curtailed when Turpin, who was apparently a dreadful shot, accidentally hit King while trying to assist his escape after King had been arrested while collecting a stabled horse that Turpin had previously stolen. Turpin's poor aim proved fatal, but before King died he managed to furnish the constables with enough information to force Turpin to flee to Yorkshire by way of evading capture. In the north he settled under the false name of John Palmer and financed a high style of living by continuing to rustle livestock and committing the occasional highway robbery. Returning disgruntled one day from an unsuccessful hunt, 'Palmer' shot his landlord's cockerel, then threatened the landlord himself when he remonstrated over the loss of his prizefighting cock. Taken into custody and held in York Castle Gaol, Turpin was subsequently convicted after a positive identification was made by chance. Turpin had written a letter to his brother-in-law who had refused to pay the sixpence postage due and consequently the correspondence was returned to the post office where, by a sheer twist of fate, Turpin's former schoolmaster,

Mr Smith, saw it and recognised the handwriting. Smith also claimed the reward on Turpin's head, which today would be the equivalent of £30,000.

Between his sentence and execution, Turpin's cell was frequently filled with visitors. In preparation for his execution he bought new clothes and shoes, and also hired five mourners at 10s each.

On 7 April 1739, Dick Turpin was conveyed through the streets of York in an open cart, bowing to the crowds that lined the route along Castlegate, over the Ouse Bridge and on along Ousegate, before continuing up the steep slope of Micklegate. He was driven underneath Micklegate's bar and onto Blossom Street, past The Mount and finally reaching the Knavesmire, where Turpin faced his ultimate date with the noose.

After climbing the ladder to the gallows with a firm step, Turpin then spent half an hour chatting to the executioner and guards. Turpin's bravado did not fail him, as reported in the *York Courant*, 'With undaunted courage looked about him, and after speaking a few words to the topsman, he threw himself off the ladder and expired in about five minutes.'

Dick Turpin's cell, York Castle Museum.

John Palmer/Dick Turpin's grave in St George's churchyard.

In spite of being buried in a deep grave in the churchyard of St George's, Turpin's body was later found disinterred and in the garden of one of the city surgeons. However, the thieves were thwarted as after keeping Turpin's body in the Blue Boar Inn overnight (in those days a public house often had a room that was used as a temporary mortuary), to prevent any further 'body snatching' attempts Turpin was re-buried in St George's churchyard, this time the coffin was filled with unslacked quicklime.

'The Glamorous Highwayman': John 'Swift Nick' Nevison

John (also known as William) Nevison was renowned as one of the most flamboyant highwaymen in the litany of England's thieving highway rogues. A charming man of tall, gentlemanly appearance, his exploits even gained the notice of King Charles II who allegedly nicknamed Nevison 'Swift Nick'.

Swift Nick's escapades are the subject of confused and conflicting accounts, although the overnight ride to York mistakenly attributed to Dick Turpin seems to be founded in fact. At 4 a.m. on a summer's morning in 1676, Nevison robbed a traveller on the highway at Gads Hill in Kent. Mounted on a bay mare, he crossed the Thames by ferry and travelled on to Chelmsford, where he rested his horse for half an hour before riding through Cambridge and Huntingdon until he met the Great North Road and headed for York. Arriving at sunset, he stabled his exhausted horse after the 200-mile journey – considered an impossible journey at that time – and proceeded to secure himself an unquestionable alibi. After washing and changing into clean clothes, Nevison made his way to the bowling green where he knew the Lord Mayor of York was playing – what better upstanding witness could he have chosen to converse with – and also laid a wager on the outcome of the match, placing his bet at eight o'clock that evening. Nevison was later arrested for the Gads Hill hold-up, but producing the Lord Mayor as witness in his defence ensured that a verdict of 'not guilty' was returned, as well as propelling him into folk history.

While Nevison's romantic reputation seems to be based on the claim that he never used violence against those he robbed, the death of a constable named Fletcher, who died while trying to arrest him, was ultimately Nevison's undoing. After this incident, he was targeted by bounty hunters before finally being arrested – his whereabouts were given away by the landlady of the Three Houses Inn at Sandal Magna, near Wakefield. Nevison had been previously arrested and made his escape on numerous occasions (when arrested in 1681 he escaped by feigning death and an accomplice masquerading as a doctor pronounced him dead from plague, which gave rise to the tales that Nevison's ghost was perpetrating further highway robberies), however, this was the end of the road for Swift Nick. After making a farewell speech to the large crowd, Nevison was hanged at the York Tyburn on Saturday, 4 May 1684 and buried at St Mary's Church, Castlegate, in an unmarked grave.

The Forest Of Galtres: 'Haunted by Robbers'

The royal Forest of Galtres was ancient woodland that once extended right up to the city walls of York, the possible sylvan remnants of which are still present in Rawcliffe Meadows. In 1870, John Marius Wilson described how the forest was once 'tenanted by wild beasts, and haunted by robbers; was the scene of many and frequent perils and exploits.' The forest was thought to be so treacherous that patrols were sent out from Bootham Bar, the northern entrance to the city, to guide travellers and protect them from

The lantern tower at All Saints' Church.

The Burton Stone.

the marauding packs of wolves, bandits and robbers therein. The fifteenth-century lantern tower of All Saints' Church on the Pavement was built especially in order to house a lamp that was kept burning to guide the way for those approaching York through the gloaming of Galtres.

Also, at the corner of Burton Stone Lane stood the chapel of St Mary Magdalen, where travellers would pray for safe passage and guidance through the forest. In front of the Burton Stone Inn is the Burton Stone itself, enclosed by iron railings, marking the limit of the old jurisdiction of the city and a reminder that in 1604, over 3,500 people died in a violent outbreak of plague in the city; the Burton Stone was used as a point for quarantined food exchange in an effort to limit infection.

Gibbeting in Galtres

As an example to other would-be highway robbers, the body of Barnhard Siegfred was hung in chains in the Forest at Stockton (the village of

Stockton on the Forest was originally a settlement that was established in a clearing in the Forest of Galtres) after being hanged for highway robbery and the attempted murder of one Master John Dolland on a dark winter's evening in December 1570. Clearly the example was not grim enough, as on Saturday, 27 June 1574 a gang of robbers were executed at the York Tyburn for wounding with intent to murder Baron de Cavallo as he was returning through the forest on his way back from Penrith. The bodies of gang members Robert de Fleury, George de Abbott and William de Abbott were not gibbeted, instead their bodies were given over to the city surgeons for dissection.

On Saturday, 29 March 1615, Mark Trumble and Robert Martinson were hanged at the Knavesmire for highway robbery in the Forest of Galtres, near the village of Shipton. Martinson was a native of Haxby, a neighbouring forest village, and Trumble was from Ripon. Both were buried in the churchyard of St Olave's (pronounced 'Olive') in Marygate.

A number of 'noteworthy' highwaymen were also apprehended in the forest, with the execution of 'daring highwayman' Amos Lawson attracting a sizeable crowd – the Knavesmire resembled 'more a fair for business

'his nose was cut off'

and pleasure than a place of execution' when he was hanged on Wednesday, 30 July 1644. Lawson had been operating as a highway robber for some time, but was at last captured in the Forest of Galtres on the night of 3 April, when he made the mistake of attempting to rob Willam Taylor, the Sheriff of York. Lawson was buried in the churchyard of St George's.

Jeremiah Balderson and Richard Souly were two other notorious highwaymen who were apprehended after the aggravated robbery of George Melrose when he was travelling through the forest on the night of 3 February 1661. Not only was Melrose robbed, but his nose was cut off as well. Balderson and Souly were hanged on Saturday, 19 August – however, they escaped the fate of dissection and were buried in Holy Trinity, Curia Regis.

Possibly not as visually arresting as a gibbeted body, but certainly an enduring reminder, the Nichol's Stone commemorates a highway robber who was hanged at York for theft and murder committed on a stretch of

The Nichol's Stone, or the 'Murder Stone' as it is known.

the A684 known as Conyers Lane, between Constable Burton and Patrick Brompton. Inscribed with the words, 'May 19, 1826 Do No Murder', this ashlar sandstone slab reputedly relates to the death of Nicholas Carter of Crakehall, who was robbed and murdered on the spot by Leonard Wilkinson. Carter had been seen by Wilkinson driving some livestock to Leyburn market that May morning in 1826. Lying in wait and waylaying Carter on his return journey in order to steal the pocket full of money his cattle had made at sale, Wilkinson was subsequently brought to justice and hanged at the New Drop on Monday, 17 July 1826. His body was brought back and buried in unconsecrated ground outside the churchyard of Finghall Church, a stone's throw from where his crime was committed and where he is said to have sought sanctuary for some time.

Known locally as the 'Murder Stone', during work to widen the carriageway on this stretch of A-road some twenty years ago, it was found necessary to relocate the stone to a position further back on the verge. To this day, however, those passing Nichol's Stone on particularly dark, moonless nights, and aware of its grim history, report feeling an eerie foreboding about the route taken by the lifeless corpse of Wilkinson making his final journey from York's gallows to his unconsecrated grave.

CHAPTER TEN
POISONOUS PERPETRATORS

To use poison as a murder weapon takes planning and some degree of skill, a poisoner could never claim that the crime was committed in the 'heat of the moment', which makes this premeditated attack seem more controlled and sinister.

Poison became a popular method of killing in medieval times, as the increase in the establishment of apothecary shops in many towns and cities offered the sale of substances for medicinal use that could be employed for more malign purposes. After all, as nineteenth-century toxicologist Alfred Swaine Taylor is quoted as saying, 'A poison in a small dose is a medicine, a medicine in a large dose is a poison.'

Before the development of analytical chemistry increased the risk that a poisoner would be caught, it was popularly seen as a method of murder more frequently employed by females. As it required no physical exertion, the lady of the house was ideally placed to conveniently administer a poison, because they were predominantly involved with the preparation of food and the household management of remedies and medicines. However, as we shall see, the balance of past poisoners is very far from being gender specific.

Since aconite has earned the sobriquet of 'Queen of Poisons', arsenic should surely be crowned 'King' since it has probably claimed more lives than any other poison. William Farr, the Statistic Head of the General Register Office in 1840, said, 'It is generally asked for to kill "rats", but it is questionable whether arsenic kills more rats than human beings.' In France, arsenic came to be called *poudre de succession*, meaning 'inheritance powder'. Perhaps its popularity lay in its virtual tastelessness with a cumulative effect acting particularly on the liver and kidneys – it could be administered in small doses over a span of time until a critical level was reached. Conveniently for the murderer, the symptoms of arsenic poisoning closely resembled those of cholera, as well as those of dysentery, and as a result many murders went undetected. In the past, arsenic was administered as a yellow-coloured sulphide, however, the white oxide form derived from metallic ore was progressively employed, which induced symptoms such as irritation and burning to the throat, faintness, nausea and vomiting mucous flecked with blood. Progressive abdominal pain, respiratory constriction and a white 'furry' covering to the tongue signalled that within the next twelve to eighteen hours severe diarrhoea and a weakened, irregular pulse would cause collapse and result in death. Not a good way to go.

Eventually, because of the level of murder cases in the nineteenth century involving the poison, the Government was forced to introduce the Arsenic Act in 1851, forbidding the sale of any arsenic compounds to a purchaser who was unknown to the supplying pharmacist. Would-be poisoners were further thwarted by the introduction of a requirement that all manufacturers of arsenic powder mix 1oz of a colouring agent (indigo or soot were employed) to every 1lb of arsenic powder produced.

However, before this legislation was introduced, there were many murders committed using this particular poison. In the case of Hannah Whitley, a pie was used to deliver the fatal dose of arsenic, with the poison concentrated in the crust. Hannah claimed she had been coerced into the act of poisoning her employer, and certainly her culinary efforts had the desired effect as her pastry made the entire Rhodes family ill, and ultimately killed five-year-old John Rhodes.

In her defence, Hannah claimed that a man named Horseman, a local linen weaver, had forced her to put the poison into the food, threatening to kill her if she refused (Rhodes and Horseman were involved in an on-going feud), and Rhodes' children were not the intended victims. Nonetheless, while Horseman faced no formal proceedings, it was Hannah who paid the penalty with her life. She was hanged at the York Tyburn on 3 August 1789.

Twenty-two-year-old William Smith employed an ingenious and indeed seasonal method of administering arsenic to poison not only his stepfather but his two half-siblings as well. William's mother had re-married Thomas Harper, who already had two children of his own, William and Anne. Faced with the ultimate division and diminution of his inheritance, Smith purchased two pennyworth of arsenic from the local apothecary, whose suspicions he failed to arouse because he also purchased some remedies for his horses at the same time, and allegedly had a problem with rats in his barn.

Smith decided the perfect way to administer the poison would be to mix it with the ingredients of the Good Friday cake that was being prepared for the household. But, unbeknownst to Smith, a maid-servant had seen him interfering with the flour.

The Harpers' neighbours had been invited over to partake of the Easter treat too, but clearly providence was on their side when they were unable to make dinner, and as it turned out only Tom Harper and his two children ended up eating any of the fatal cake.

As soon as the poison began to take effect Smith fled to Liverpool, leaving his victims to suffer in agony until father and both children died the following day. In spite of the motives that had driven Smith's actions, he found he was unable to live with his crime, and returned home, where he was immediately apprehended and confessed all.

At the Autumn Assizes of 1753, Smith's own confession, along with the evidence of the apothecary and the maid-servant, ensured he was found

'leaving his victims to suffer in agony'

guilty and sentenced to death. On Monday 15 August, Smith was hanged at the Tyburn and afterwards his body was sent for dissection.

As previously mentioned, the symptoms of arsenic poisoning closely resembled those of cholera, and while this masked many murders, it proved to be Ursula Lofthouse's undoing and would see her swing at the New Drop.

Twenty-six-year-old Ursula was married to Robert Lofthouse, with whom she had a sixteen-month-old child. She poisoned her husband with two pennyworth of arsenic purchased from the local druggist, Mr Harland, in Kirkby Malzeard. On returning home from market one evening in early November 1834, the hungry Robert asked his wife to boil him some potatoes, but she had already made a cake for his tea, which was promptly consumed. The effects of the poison were immediate, but it was initially assumed that Robert had contracted cholera. He continued to vomit until Saturday morning and the doctor, who had been summoned the afternoon before, forty-eight hours after ingestion, could do nothing to stop it. Clearly Ursula was set on her purpose and persuaded her husband to take some more food and she spread treacle on the remainder of the fateful cake; this had the desired effect and Robert Lofthouse died soon afterwards.

Ursula might have escaped detection if it hadn't been for her brother-in-law Henry's concern. The supposed cause of his brother's death was having a detrimental effect on his business, which led him to consider the suspicious circumstances surrounding it. The fear of cholera was making customers desert his shop, and he, therefore, instigated an investigation into Robert's death.

Mr Dinsdale, a coroner of York, assisted by John Buckle, a surgeon from Bedale, examined the body of the deceased. They committed a thorough examination of the stomach contents and after consulting an eminent chemist from Leeds, named Mr West, they concluded that there was a presence of 'white arsenic in a quantity sufficient enough to produce death'. A further 'nail in the coffin' of Ursula's initial protested innocence was the fact that four chickens that had pecked at some of Lofthouse's vomit also died, and evidence of arsenic was found in the craw of each bird. The finger of suspicion was now firmly pointed in Ursula's direction.

The conversation on the custodial journey to York certainly helped imply her guilt – eighteen miles from Kirkby she revealed certain facts to local constable Thomas Thorpe, into whose custody she was being transferred. Thorpe testified at Ursula's trial, stating that, 'The prisoner began to talk about her husband. She said he had a disagreeable breath; that he would hardly allow her common necessaries to live; that she believed he had saved between £40 and £50 and that he never told her what he did with his money; that she believed he carried it to Henry Lofthouse, and that he loved Ellen Lofthouse better than her, which made her very unhappy.'

On 6 April 1835, Ursula Lofthouse was hanged alongside two other convicted murderers, Joseph Healy and William Allott, in a triple execution that marked the end of the thirty-three-year career of John Curry, one of York's notable hangmen.

There was no question that Ann Barber had poisoned her husband James with the pennyworth of white arsenic she had purchased on the day of the murder, allegedly to 'poison mice'. Apparently, Ann had been 'esteemed handsome in her youth' and had been educated among the Ranters – an anarchic religious sect of extremists who were generally held by the established Church to be lacking in 'moral values or restraint in worldly pleasures'. Whether this education had a bearing on Ann's moralistic views in later life we cannot know. She was happily married to James Barber for some fifteen years, until the arrival of a lodger, William Thompson, in their marital home. The subsequent affair between Thompson and Mrs Barber resulted in Ann leaving her husband and co-habiting with Thompson, although the couple only lived together for one week, after which time Ann returned to her husband, on 4 January 1821. We can conclude that matrimonial harmony was not fully restored to the Barbers, because by the 16 March Ann had poisoned her husband.

At her trial, when the jury gave their verdict of 'guilty', it was noted that:

She did not seem conscious of the result of the trial; but when asked in the usual form, what she had to say why sentence of death should not be passed upon her, she became sensible of her dreadful situation, trembled exceedingly, shrieked, and fell upon the floor near the bar. She was raised by the jailor, and supported herself by taking hold of the iron bar in front, and leaning backwards and forward in great agitation.

Executed on Monday, 30 August 1821 at the New Drop, Ann 'received spiritual consolation, and died without a struggle' – she left behind two children, aged sixteen and ten.

However, the murder of Thomas Hodgson could be equally attributed to the victim's gullibility as well as the poisonous pills supplied to him by an ex-employee, one Michael Simpson. Protesting his innocence and claiming that the pills he had supplied Hodgson with had been given to him by a 'wise man', whose identity could not be revealed. Simpson's theft of £100 from the deceased may have had some bearing on his motives.

Thomas Hodgson, owner of the profitable limekilns in Crakehall, was described as a 'resolute and rash man' and seemed to have ample capacity for making enemies, as demonstrated when a horse belonging to one of his neighbours strayed on to his land – Hodgson killed the poor animal with an axe. It is possible that Simpson just held a grudge against his former employer, and that the burglary and subsequent poisoning of Hodgson at Theakston Grange was an act of revenge on his part. Simpson had called by on the pretence of enquiring after his former master's health and to let the Hodgsons know that he had seen that some of their livestock had strayed and were in difficulty. Mrs Hodgson went to investigate as her husband was feeling unwell and was indisposed at the time, and while Simpson initially accompanied Mrs Hodgson to help with the stock, he very soon gave her the slip (presumably to return to the house and steal the £100 from underneath the Hodgsons' mattress). On reaching the 'strayed' cows, Mrs Hodgson discovered that the cattle had been deliberately driven into the ditch.

Some days after this incident, Simpson again called by to console with the Hodgsons over the dreadful theft of their money. He then went on to say that he had been to see a wise man who had given him two pills, and if Mr Hodgson were to swallow them that night with nothing further to eat

and then walk in the garden, the identity of the robber would be magically revealed and all the stolen money returned to him! The prospect of regaining his wealth clearly overrode common sense and Mr Hodgson was very soon afterwards taken 'dreadfully ill', and 'vomited much, complained of violent pains and expired the same night'. One might think that to believe in such a foolhardy suggestion as magic pills is quite ridiculous, even in a superstitious age, but Thomas Hodgson clearly wished to see the return of his money by any means, no matter how implausible. Simpson was hanged on Monday, 17 March 1801 at the York Tyburn.

Oxalic acid was the poison of choice for two murderous sisters, Elizabeth and Helen Drysdale, aged twenty-six and twenty-four respectively, who were executed on Saturday, 10 April 1647, at the gallows of St Leonard's. They were sentenced to death for the wilful and deliberate murder of Robert Boss from Heslington, near York, and Robert Blanchard of Walmgate in the city. The sisters had poisoned both men at the home of Dame Robinson, at the Sign of the Maypole Inn in Clifton, a suburb of York about a mile and half from the city centre. It was stated at their trial that the sisters were in fact courting both of the men, and just two days after St Valentine's Day 1647, the two were quite unsuspecting of the fact that the Drysdale sisters had dosed them with oxalic acid, which they had purchased that morning from the chemist shop of Mr William Brooks in Stonegate, York. Heslington and Blanchard were both dead within an hour and a half of being poisoned, though strangely before they died both freely forgave Elizabeth and Helen for what they had done.

The details as to the motive of this case are scant to say the least, all we can be certain of is that after sentence of death was passed both sisters met their fate 'with more than womanly fortitude', leaving behind a father, mother, four brothers and two sisters. After execution both sisters were given over to the city surgeons for dissection.

William Dove murdered his wife Harriet by poisoning her with strychnine stolen from a surgeon's office. Harriet was of a delicate constitution, and Dove's motive appeared to be the avoidance of further doctor's bills and possibly to give him the freedom to marry another woman. For a whole week Dove watched the agonies of his wife – he had administered the strychnine five times, and with the sixth dose he finally killed Harriet on 1 March 1856. One of the more popular poisons still in use at the start of the twentieth century (Agatha Christie's first murder mystery, the *Mysterious Affair at Styles* published in 1916, used strychnine as the murder weapon), the correct dose of strychnine can kill a person inside twenty minutes – though not in Harriet's case – after they have suffered agonising contortions and death throes; strychnine acts by attacking the central nervous system.

Dove's plea of insanity was rejected by the court, but the extent of media coverage generated by this particular trial sparked a subsequent debate over the use of medical and psychiatric evidence in trials. Dove was hanged at noon on Saturday, 9 August 1856 before an estimated record-breaking crowd of 15,000 to 20,000 onlookers.

CHAPTER ELEVEN

DEVOUT
DETAINEES

English history is peppered with religiously incited insurrections. Lollardy, a major manifestation of theological radicalism in England inspired by the writings of fourteenth-century Bible translator John Wycliffe, culminated in the unsuccessful Lollard Rebellion of 1415. However, it wasn't until the Reformation and subsequent Dissolution of the Monasteries, instigated by Henry VIII that such a strength of feeling would once again mobilise itself into mass protestation, one that was born in the heart of York.

The Pilgrimage of Grace

Laws passed in the 1530s, which reduced the influence of the Catholic Church, paved the way for the Dissolution of the Monasteries, with York feeling the impact more than most. The city had long benefited from its powerful religious links as the seat of the Archbishop of York and as the home to York Minster, as well as St Mary's Abbey, though the largest of the city's religious houses were not alone as Holy Trinity Priory, St Leonard's Hospital, St Andrew's Priory, Clementhorpe Nunnery and four friars' convents were also to suffer in the schism. Small surprise then that the religious rebellion mounted in the face of this threat, known as the Pilgrimage of Grace, began in York

After the King's Church Commissioners reached York in 1536, the first religious houses to fall were Clementhorpe Nunnery and Holy Trinity Priory in Micklegate, which were dissolved that summer.

Following the revolt led by expelled monks from the Yorkshire town of Beverley in October 1536, Yorkshire lawyer and landowner Robert Aske dubbed the rising the Pilgrimage of Grace, and rode at the head of about 5,000 horsemen through York to the minster. Here, Aske posted an order that restored all those banished monks and nuns to their former religious houses. A further 10,000 men were mustered by Sir Thomas Percy and the Abbot of St Mary's Abbey, who rode through York on their way to join Aske at Pontefract. Negotiations that December eventually brought about a royal pardon and the rebellion seemed to be over. However, when further uprisings broke out in the New Year, Aske was arrested on charges of treason and sent back to York for execution. The Pilgrimage of Grace was over for good. After execution on 12 July 1537, Aske's body was taken to a blacksmith's in the Pavement, where it was riveted in chains before being suspended from a 35-foot-high gibbet on Heworth Moor.

When King Henry VIII visited York four years later on the 15 September, (Aske's bones were still hanging in chains, a stark reminder in an age of religious intolerance) the contrite mayor, along with his aldermen and councillors, joined with the kneeling common crowd at Fulford Cross to greet Henry and his latest wife, Katherine Howard. The men promised that they were 'from the bottoms of their stomach repentant', a sentiment that was sweetened with the obsequious gifts of silver gilt cups containing £100 in gold for the King and £40 for Katherine.

In spite of 'Bloody Mary' Tudor's attempts to reinstate the Catholic Church during her brief but zealous reign, the eradication of Catholicism remained firmly on the agenda of the Protestant Elizabeth I. From their exile on the continent, some ardent Catholics were devising ways to bring England back into the fold of the old faith. By the 1570s, their efforts had percolated as far as York, and at a time when war with Catholic Spain was a real possibility, York's hard-line Catholic community was considered to be a serious problem. Termed as 'recusants', convictions of these nonconformist Roman Catholics had surged in

Fulford Cross.

number and this may well have been the impetus for using Monk Bar as a prison in 1577, as well as the new prison built on the King's Staith in 1585. York Castle was also used to hold those unable to pay their fines, most of whom were women, and of the thirty recusant wives or widows imprisoned more than a third died from disease in the squalid conditions.

Crimes of Conscience

Margaret Clitherow (née Middleton) was born in York in 1553 and baptised in the Protestant faith in St Martin-le-Grand Church. She was married at the age of fifteen in a Protestant ceremony to John Clitherow, a prosperous butcher some years her senior. However, in 1571 Margaret converted to Catholicism, on the encouragement of the wife of Dr Thomas Vavasour, a prominent York Catholic. This turn of events led to her first spell of imprisonment in 1577 for failing to attend church. Two subsequent incarcerations followed at York Castle, the second term of imprisonment lasting for twenty months, during which time Margaret learned to read.

In 1581, an act was passed outlawing Catholic religious ceremonies; it also made sheltering a Catholic priest a criminal offence punishable by death. As a consequence, between 1582 and 1583 five priests were put to death in York at the Tyburn on Knavesmire. On gaining her liberty, Margaret began to make night-time pilgrimages to the gallows. She also created a secret room in her house in the Shambles, which was used

'Punishable by death'

as a refuge for Catholic priests. However, during a raid on the house in March 1586, a frightened boy revealed the location of this secret room and it was discovered that the Clitherow house had been utilised for the instruction of local children in the Catholic faith, as well as being used to shelter priests and hold Mass. On 14 March 1586, four days after her arrest, Margaret was tried at the Guildhall, where she refused to plead; to do so would have condemned all those whom she had schooled in the faith and was, therefore, a very brave act. The penalty for not plead-ing was *peine forte et dure*, a method of execution where the accused was

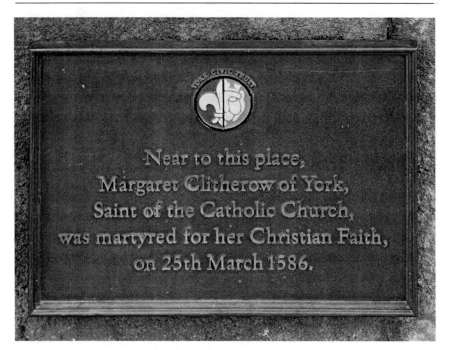

A plaque marking the spot of Margaret Clitherow's execution.

placed under a board or a door, upon which stones were then heaped until the defendent spoke up or died. The following day, Margaret was held in prison on Ouse Bridge, deprived of food and allowed only puddle water to drink until she was eventually taken to the Toll Booth and executed on the 25 March. She was crushed beneath eight hundred pounds of rock, which caused her ribs to break through the skin. It took fifteen minutes for Margaret Clitherow to die; her last words are reported to have been, 'Jesu, Jesu, Jesu, have mercy on me!'

Margaret's body was then unceremoniously dumped on one of the city's public dunghills. However, some six weeks later, her body was exhumed by a group of dedicated Catholics who gave Margaret a Christian burial, minus her hand which remains preserved as a holy relic at the Bar Convent in York to this day. Margaret Clitherow was canonized by Pope Paul VI in 1970 and also endowed as the patron saint of the Catholic Women's League. A statue of Margaret can be found in the church of St Wilfrid in High Petergate, close to the minster.

Guy Fawkes

'A rope, a rope, to hang the Pope, a penn'orth of cheese to choke him, a pint of beer to wash it down, And a jolly good fire to roast him.' Some lines from the well-known rhyme, 'Remember, remember! The fifth of November,

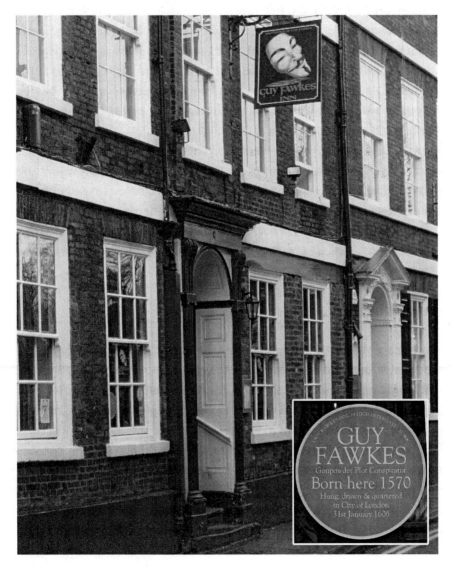

The Guy Fawkes Inn, High Petergate.

the Gunpowder treason and plot.' In the thirteen years prior to 1595, thirty Catholic priests were tried and executed in the north of England, most of whom met their end at York's Knavesmire. It was during these years of religious intolerance that a Protestant York schoolboy was converted to Catholicism – his name was Guy Fawkes.

Born on 13 April 1570 to Edward and Edith Fawkes, Guy was baptised at St Michael Belfry and was raised as a Protestant. In 1578, when he was eight years old, Guy's father died. Edith lived on as a widow for nine years, however, in 1587 she re-married and both she and Guy relocated to the village of Scotton, about twenty miles from York. It was here that the teen-aged Guy was heavily influenced by his step-father, laying the foundations for his subsequent conversion to Catholicism.

At the age of twenty-three, Fawkes left English soil as a converted Catholic and fought for Catholic Spain in the Eighty Years' War, and it was at this time that he adopted the name 'Guido' and gained his expertise in the use of explosives. The rest is history, as they say, and now annually on the 5th November effigies of Guy are burnt on bonfires – although, tradition says that the citizens of York are not supposed to burn Guy on this day, in deference to his status as a son of the city.

The Quakers

George Fox (1624–91) was a travelling shoemaker who founded the Society of Friends, or Quakers as they became known. Preaching throughout the Midlands and the north of England, his denunciations that people should communicate directly with God instead of through the intermediary of a corrupt church landed him in prison twice. One of his earliest converts in the county of Yorkshire, Thomas Aldam, was also the first of many Quakers imprisoned in York Castle for their religious principles.

Committed to gaol in 1652, Adlam remained a prisoner for about two and a half years, during which time his wife and family were frequently denied visiting rights. During this particular confinement Adlam was brought before Judge Parker, where he declined to remove his hat on conscientious motives and insisted on addressing the judge as 'thee' instead of 'you'. This conduct cost Adlam dearly and he was fined £40 and committed to prison until the fine was paid. However, on application to Oliver Cromwell, the Lord Protector of the Commonwealth granted an order for Adlam's liberation.

In 1651, George Fox had travelled to York, two days before what he termed as 'the time called Christmas', as he was commanded by the Lord to go to the minster to do his bidding. The following is taken from his autobiography:

York Minster steps, the scene of Fox's enforced tumble.

Speak to priest Bowles and his hearers in their great cathedral. Accordingly I went. When the priest had done, I told them I had something from the Lord God to speak to the priest and people. 'Then say on quickly' said a professor, for there was frost and snow, and it was very cold weather. Then I told them that this was the Word of the Lord God unto them – that they lived in words, but God Almighty looked for fruits amongst them.

As soon as the words were out of my mouth, they hurried me out, and threw me down the steps. But I got up again without hurt, and went to my lodging.

Probably the only religious founder to have ever been thrown down the steps of York Minster, Fox was lucky to escape with only the odd bump and bruise, as opposed to being sent for another spell in York Castle, or suffering the fate of some of his staunchly persecuted forebears, who paid with their lives for adhering to their religious constancy.

CHAPTER TWELVE

CARNAL CRIMES

The Oldest Profession

Throughout England's history, the illegality of prostitution seemingly did nothing to diminish the demand for the services of 'fallen women', or have a detrimental effect on the level of street-walkers and brothel-keepers over the centuries, and it was the same in York as anywhere else.

While the presence and scale of prostitution in a seemingly genteel cathedral city such as York may seem surprising, the industrial boom that built up cities like Leeds, Bradford and Sheffield, offering employment opportunities for women as well as men, for the most part passed York by, and with the rapid population increase in the first half of the nineteenth century, prostitution provided a means to an end. However, records indicate that certain areas of York, such as the central part of the walled city, were concentrated areas for harlotry and brothels since the Middle Ages, long before the advent of the pressing overcrowding of the Victorian era.

Grape Lane, York.

The Blue Bicycle Restaurant in Fossgate. Today, the presence of the Blue Bicycle outside the premises indicates service of the culinary kind.

Today's Grape Lane, just a stone's throw from the minster and linking Petergate with Swinegate, was once a dark alley called 'Grapecuntlane' – grape originally meaning to grope, the rest of the interpretation I leave to the reader and their own sensibilities! It was normal practice for a medieval street name to reflect its economic activity or function, and adjacent to Grape Lane is Finkle Street, a thoroughfare of similarly indecent reputation that as late as the nineteenth century was still known as 'Murky (or Mucky) Peg Lane'. Another acknowledged centre of prostitution was St Andrewsgate, where the partially derelict church of St Andrew was given over to use as a brothel in the sixteenth century (St Andrews has since reverted back to its original more orthodox usage and is now home to the York Brethren Assembly).

Now known as something of a dining landmark, the Blue Bicycle Restaurant in York's Fossgate is so named because at the turn of the last century the cellar was employed as a brothel of some repute. The lady owner of this establishment always rode a blue bicycle, and when the bicycle was propped against the wall outside her premises, clients would know that the brothel was open for business.

Street Girls

Perhaps not as salubrious as Fossgate, the Waters lanes of the city was then a collection of dark, overcrowded, filthy tenements and was populated with those forced by circumstance into thieving and prostitution.

Isabella Campbell and Caroline Nicholson were two such 'street girls' from Middle Water Lane, both aged around nineteen and already known to the police. Isabella and Caroline were described as 'resembling the lower and more degrading class of street walker' with their coercion of one unwilling client resulting in murder.

On a December evening in 1853, upon returning from the York Horse Show – the once nationally renowned sale always held in the last full week before Christmas – the rather inebriated John Hall was weaving his way back to his lodgings after selling his horse at the market, and celebrating the successful sale in the White Swan enroute, a coaching inn on the Pavement.

Hall's advanced state of drunkenness was clearly evident to the girls, who obviously decided he was an easy mark. Isabella and Caroline accosted him, one on each side, and led Hall onto the Staith, the street skirting the banks of the Ouse, and headed toward their lodgings. However, as Hall's reluctance became apparent, the girls changed tactic, and in their attempts to search his overcoat in order to steal his purse, John Hall was edged further towards the river's edge. As Hall's protestations and refusal to give up his money

Water Lane in 1853, by Francis Bedford. (Courtesy of York Museums Trust, York Art Gallery)

The King's Staith, next to today's waterside.

increased, Isabella, with very little effort, pushed the unfortunate man into the icy winter waters.

The girls made a sharp exit onto Ouse Bridge, but Police Constable Catton, who was patrolling the vicinity that evening, noticed the guilty pair pass as they made for McGregor's Dram Shop on Low Ousegate. The constable's attention was then drawn by the uproar of a crowd that had gathered after the commotion, some of who had witnessed Hall's subsequent fall into the river. Hall was beyond rescue, however, and his body was found later that evening some 500 feet downstream, close to the public washing area known as 'Pudding Holes'. One of the onlookers was able to positively identify Isabella and Caroline though, and when PC Catton caught up with them and arrested them both on the corner of Nessgate, Campbell and Nicholson were taken into custody. While at the station, they were searched by another police officer's wife (as was procedure), and a purse was found on Isabella Campbell's person.

The following day, when the girls appeared before the magistrates at the Guildhall, they were ordered to be remanded in the House of Correction at Toft's Green, near Micklegate Bar. The coroner's inquest the following day sealed their fates as it was put to the jury that the girls had wilfully pushed John Hall into the river while trying to rob him, and were, therefore, guilty of murder. If Hall had been physically cajoled while the girls were trying to persuade him in the direction of their lodgings then this would only be deemed as manslaughter; after a deliberation of just one hour the jury returned a verdict of 'wilful murder'.

Punishing Prostitution

Methods of visible chastisement were the favoured punishments for prostitution, including branding, whipping, ear clipping, nose slitting and shaving off their hair. As an additional penalty, prostitutes were forbidden to wear aprons, as this garment was regarded as the mark of a 'respectable woman'. In 1513, a proclamation was made that prostitutes be punished by branding on the face, thereby ensuring that any future entry into respectable society would be impossible. In 1623, this 'Branding Act' was extended so that 'any woman convicted of taking goods valued at more than twelvepence would suffer, in addition to a whipping or other punishment, the branding of a letter 'T' with a hot burning iron on her left thumb.' The penalty of branding was often carried out immediately after a sentence had been given, to ensure that the officiating magistrates could witness 'the smoke from the offender's singed skin to prevent a less than scalding hot iron from being used in return for a bribe.'

As was the case with adulterers and slanderers, public shaming was an integral part of the chastisement process, with prostitutes, bawds and scolds taken in open carts to the place of punishment.

Brothel keepers were also subject to prosecution and punishable by branding on the face. Keeping a house of ill repute, where prostitution was encouraged, was an offence, as was the misdemeanour of keeping a 'molly house' for 'sodomitical practices'. Under the Buggery Act of 1533, buggery (in law, a term often interchangeable with sodomy) was deemed a capital offence in England. However, prosecution of homosexuality was not restricted to the confines of these molly houses, as the case and ultimate execution of thirty-two-year-old Thomas Rogers attests, when he was hanged for an 'unnatural crime' on Saturday, 26 April 1834.

The period from 1828 to 1836 saw the end of capital punishment for crimes other than murder and attempted murder, and after 1836 these were the only crimes, in practice, attracting the death penalty. However, when Rogers committed the crime of sodomy with his fellow servant George Bennett (aged fourteen years) in 1834, it was still deemed a capital offence. During this time, prosecutions for homosexuality accounted for 2 per cent of the overall executions in England.

Unnatural Crimes

The Buggery Act also covered the offence of bestiality – a crime for which seventy-seven-year-old John Hoyland was controversially tried and executed in 1793. One newspaper at the time termed the accusation as 'A crime we cannot name'. But it seems, in all probability, that the accusation made against John Hoyland was entirely false and generated by the motivation of 'blood money'.

Hoyland, who was described as a 'simple, apparently harmless man', had raised a large family in what was then rural Attercliffe, who were in turn unkindly described as 'scarcely removed from a state of idiocy, and some of them dumb.' Sadly, Hoyland had been the victim of appalling domestic violence instigated by his sons, who would often beat their father so severely that he 'frequently was weeks together with bruises on him.'

On the day of the alleged offence, 15 July 1793, two Sheffield labourers, William Warburton and John Hunt, stated that they had seen Hoyland

'Victim of appalling domestic violence'

coupling with an ass. At this time, there were statutes in existence, offering financial reward to anyone instrumental in prosecuting a felon to conviction, hence the term 'blood money'. Not surprisingly this system was open to abuse, and in this instance, as the accusation was generally held to be spurious by John's neighbours, it was likely that Warburton and Hunt's motives were purely pecuniary.

John Hoyland protested his innocence up to the moment the noose was tied around his neck, and insisted to the spectators in the crowd that 'he would not change places with the men who had sworn his life away.'

While Hoyland's case acted as a catalyst for the alteration of the legislation governing 'blood money', it was not until 1818 that the fixed rewards offered on the statutes were replaced by discretionary rewards made by the court, thereby removing the assurance and lure of the prospect of 'blood money' for good.

If you enjoyed this book, you may also be interested in …

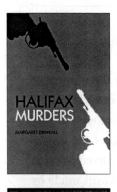

Halifax Murders

MARGARET DRINKALL

Featuring all factions of the criminal underworld, this macabre selection
of tales includes the case of a husband who boasted that he had played
'Jack the Ripper' after slitting his wife's throat, a mother who murdered
her two children and a man who was bludgeoned to death in a newspaper
office. Drawing on a wide variety of historical sources and containing many
cases which have never before been published, *Halifax Murders* will fascinate
everyone interested in true crime and the history of this West Yorkshire town.

978 0 7524 7949 1

Folklore of Yorkshire

KAI ROBERTS

The beautiful county of Yorkshire is the largest in Britain, and yet still
possesses a strong and cohesive regional identity. Discover Yorkshire's
holy wells and buried treasure, its boggarts, Black Dogs and fairies, and
the legends behind the county's stunning landscape. This fully illustrated
book shows how the customs of the past have influenced the ways of today
whilst also revealing something about the nature of folklore itself, both for
the tradition-bearers and those who collect it.

978 0 7524 8579 9

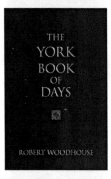

The York Book of Days

ROBERT WOODHOUSE

Taking you through the year day by day, *The York Book of Days* contains a
quirky, eccentric, amusing or important event or fact from different periods
of history, many of which had a major impact on the religious and political
history of England as a whole. Ideal for dipping into, this addictive little book
will keep you entertained and informed. Featuring hundreds of snippets of
information gleaned from the vaults of York's archives, it will delight residents
and visitors alike.

978 0 7524 6045 1

Bloody British History Leeds

RICHARD SMYTH

Leeds has one of the darkest histories on record. From the fatal Dripping
Riot of 1865, sparked by the theft of two pounds of congealed fat, to the
violin-playing killer Charles Peace, said to still haunt the city's prison cells,
you will find all manner of horrible events inside this book. With plague and
disease in the city slums, dreadful disasters in Roundhay Park, and riots in the
city centre, this is the real story of Yorkshire's first city.

978 0 7524 8737 3

Visit our website and discover thousands of other History Press books.

www.thehistorypress.co.uk

The
History
Press